T5-BQA-891

FOUNDATIONS OF INDIAN MUSICOLOGY

(Perspectives in the Philosophy of Art and Culture)

FOUNDATIONS OF INDIAN MUSICOLOGY

(Perspectives in the Philosophy of Art and Culture)

PRADIP KUMAR SENGUPTA

First published in India 1991

Publishers
Shakti Malik
Abhinav Publications
E 37, Hauz Khas
New Delhi-110 016 (INDIA)

ISBN 81-7017-273-X

Jacket Design
Herman Van Hecke, Visva Bharati, Santiniketan

Lasertypeset by
Shagun Composers
92-B, Street No. 4
Krishna Nagar
Safdarjung Enclave
New Delhi-110 029

Arun & Rajive Pvt Ltd
10 DSIDC Scheme II, Phase II
Okhla Industrial Estate
New Delhi-110 020

वीणापाणिवरप्राप्तो मार्गसंगीतसाधकः।
वन्द्योपाध्यायवंशश्रीनिखिलोऽद्य दिवंगतः।।
सौजन्यजितविश्वाय प्रियाय सुहृदे मम।
मयायं श्रद्धया तस्मै ग्रन्थो निवेद्यते मुदा।।

CONTENTS

CONTENTS

PREFACE

This book is not a study of the history of the musical heritage of India; nor is it a study of the chronological development of Indian musicology. It is a humble attempt at exploring some issues which may be regarded as constituting the foundations of Indian musicology. In this attempt I have tried to develop the philosophico-cultural and non-theistic religious presuppositions of ancient Indian music and their influence on the subsequent stages of its growth. The unavailability of the original sources of Indian musicology makes the task immensely difficult; still it appears to be worth pursuing because a constructive attempt on the basis of conceptual analysis may be of some help, however little, for us to understand the continuity of the running thread of music, the richest and perhaps the oldest tradition of the most illuminating art of India.

Indian music is said to be the enviable precious treasure of Indian culture. An assimilation of Aryan and non-Aryan cultures on the one hand and on the other of Hindu, Muslim, Indo-Iranian and Persian cultures, Indian music has grown into a full-bloom lotus which, still today, continues in its own glory emanating its ineffable ethos triumphantly conquering thousands of millions of souls in all corners of the world.

The phrase 'Indian music' is used here in the sense of 'Classical Indian music' (as prevalent in North India), the nearest English equivalent of *Mārga Sangeet* as distinguished from *Deśi Sangeet,* a terminology used by *Matangamuni* in his *Bṛhaddeśi.* Attempts have been made to establish that it is the spiritual vision of man, either the inner gift a man is fortunately born with or the gift attained by man through deep meditation or through ceaseless cultivation of the so-called hidden treasures of music, that brings out the *musician in man.*

Utmost care has been taken, with what success I do not know, to interpret the fundamental principles of Indian musicology by keeping it away from its mythological orientations. A closer study of Indian musicology would perhaps reveal the fact that either it has been overdone in the direction of deification or it has been underdone in the direction of being too cryptic. The result is that to most of the scholars it appears to be rather obscure and to some extent confusing. It is for this reason that musicology is fast losing its interest to the researchers who suffer from some sort of aversion to a serious study of this vast and important subject. This is one of the drawbacks for which musicology is not pursued as seriously as it should have been in Indian Universities. This book, however, is not meant to compensate this drawback; but researchers in this field may find some debatable and controversial issues worth further probing into.

We have tried to establish how the magical powers of musical notes in the hands of Indian musicians of dedication can do miracles in bringing man closer to each other and ultimately to the threshold of the Transcendent Eternal. But at the same time the book also denounces the utility of deification of Indian *rāgas* because this will only undermine the supreme power of musical creativity. It is rather a snag which has to be crossed over in order to realise the proper significance of Indian music.

Indian music has never been a stereotyped system of closed orthodox ideas and rules. It has already grown with new and new experiments in all the important stages of history. In this book I have tried to place the focus on the fundamental rules and conventions together with a rational interpretation of the *Rāga* system of Indian music and its aesthetic appeal with the hope that it might help the scholars and researchers to understand the subject in its proper perspective. There is also an added hope that it might go someway in unfolding the simple religion of spiritual vision where all human beings are alike irrespective of their caste and creed. This is, however, the inner secret which the music of India has particularly placed its focus on. Indian music thus may be said to be rooted in man's spiritual culture. I regret that due attention could not be given to South Indian Music in all its details; some relevant references indeed are taken into consideration. The views of Western thinkers on religion, culture and music or other forms of Art have been discussed incidentally either as parallels or as contraries in so far as they are helpful in working out the main thesis of this book.

Chapter *One* deals with the essence of religion and culture which constitutes the chief foundation of all arts. In Indian context it is said to be the basis, the fountainhead of pure music in its formative stage. The same fountainhead is said to nourish Indian Music at all subsequent stages.

Chapter *Two* deals with the various branches of Visual and Performing Art.

Chapter *Three* deals with the phenomenon of Music which is further developed into the fundamental relation between Man and Music in Chapter *Four*.

Chapter *Five* is a critical treatment of the *gharānā* system of Indian

Music which is followed by an equally critical treatment of its *Tāla* system in Chapter *Six*.

Chapter *Seven* embodies a critical analysis of the *Rāga* system of Indian Music together with its aesthetic appeal (*Rasa*).

Chapter *Eight* is a constructive interpretation of the experiments of Rabindranath on Indian Musicology.

I remain ever grateful to Dr. Kapila Vatsyayan, Secretary, Indira Gandhi National Centre for Arts, New Delhi who took great interest in this work and made all arrangements for its publication.

I had the rare fortune of being intimately associated with Late Pandit Nikhil Banerjee, the great Sitar Maestro of the present times, from our boyhood days. It was he who initiated me in music and musicology. He is no more with us to receive my gratitude on the occasion of the publication of this book. May I, therefore, take the opportunity in dedicating this book to his loving memories as a mark of respect to the departed soul.

I must acknowledge my indebtedness to Pandit Jnan Prakash Ghosh of the Sangeet Research Academy, Calcutta, to Professor Sisirkona Dhar Chowdhury, Sri Buddhadev Das Gupta, Dr. E.S. Perera (Son-in-law of Ustad Ali Akbar Khan), Late Pandit T.L. Rana, Late Professor Arun Bhattacharya, Sri Sankar Ghosh, Sri Swapan Chowdhury, Sri Anindo Chatterjee, Prof. P. Josh and numerous other friends and well-wishers for their constant help and invaluable suggestions in shaping my thoughts and ideas, and in collecting and arranging the materials of this book. I had occasions to deliver lectures at national level Seminars organised by different Indian Universities and Research Institutions the relevant portions of which I have tried to incorporate in this book.

The name of Ustad Ali Akbar Khan, the greatest Indian musician of this age, deserves special mention in this context. He had been kind enough in allowing me to participate in his informal discussions at his Calcutta residence with his friends and students and such discussions gave me many important clues enabling me to construct some of my ideas regarding the unique progressive character of Indian music. He does not know how and to what extent his casual remarks have helped me.

I am indebted to Professor Nilima Sen, *Adhyaksha, Sàngeet Bhavana* and to Professor Jayanta Chakravorty, *Adhyapaka, Kala Bhavana* of *Visva Bharati*, who have made all provisions for me to utilise the respective libraries. Professor Jayanta Chakravorty, particularly, gave me many important suggestions which I have utilised here. To Professor Biswanath Banerjee, Department of Sanskrit, Pali and Prakrit, *Visva Bharati*, I owe a great deal since he took great care in explaining to me many obscure passages of the texts on musicology. Regarding the views of Rabindranath and his revolutionary approach I learnt everything from Sri Santidev Ghosh, the direct disciple of Rabindranath and my language fails to express my gratitude to him. Sri Shyamal Sarkar, Head of the Department of English, *Visva Bharati* has helped me in numerous ways. Sri Prasanta Kumar Bhanja and Dr. Sitangsu Roy of *Sangeet Bhavana, Visva Bharati,* have helped me a lot by their inspiring discussions.

My student, Dr. (Mrs.) Santwana Majumdar, now working at the Department of Philosophy and Religion, *Visva Bharati,* and Sri Gopikrishna Das, a Ph.D. student, working under my supervision worked hard in going through the entire manuscript and suggesting important corrections for a better production.

Mrs. Rekha Sengupta, an exponent of *Bhajan* and *Nazrul-geeti*, has been the main source of my inspiration in writing this book. My indebtedness to her may be taken for granted.

Lastly to Mr. Shakti Malik of Abhinav Publications, New Delhi, I offer my heartiest thanks and gratitude for his kindly undertaking the bold risk in publishing this book which obviously would not satisfy any commercial interest.

There is no tall claim in this book. I shall be happy if it only provokes the readers.

Visva Bharati
Santiniketan
March 19, 1987

Pradip Kumar Sengupta

CHAPTER I

RELIGION, CULTURE AND ART
Man's Spiritual Universe

I

It is neither possible, nor desirable to arrive at a satisfactory definition of the term 'religion' which covers all the standard religions of the world. The effective way is to try to analyse the components of the religious phenomenon and to work out the avenues of interaction between religion and society, or between the religious attitude and its impact upon the social life of an individual which is usually believed to be reflected in what is called 'culture'.

'Culture' again is another term of which no satisfactory definition is readily available. The difficulty, whether regarding 'religion' or regarding 'culture', is that no necessary or sufficient condition can be formulated which bears a reference to the basic core-content of what we normally understand by 'religion', or by 'culture'. The increasingly vast perspective of human attitude towards Nature and Society is rather responsible for the increasing ambiguity of these terms which reduces the so-called standard definitions into meaningless absurdities.

Whether we talk of 'religion', or of 'culture', there is at least one thing which cannot be ignored, namely, the concept of 'man' as a social being. In other words, 'religion' can be regarded as a human attitude in a given social context; similar is the case with 'culture'. If we closely look into the history of religions, it will be clear that an analysis of the religious situation includes some data studied by sociology, anthropology, history, psychology and, of course, theology. But whatever be the branch of study, a religious situation can be studied for its own sake where a reference to 'culture' or 'a pattern of culture' appears to be predominantly present. Such an analysis will enable one to conclude that religion is basically a human discipline in its own right which can make useful additions to the areas of study already mentioned. To properly understand and explore this discipline one has indeed to start with an attitude of openness to what may be regarded as the 'religious reality' as it is encountered in specific social contexts.

Culture, on the other hand, can be regarded as a human value which, however, consists in a perfect equilibrium of the three fundamental values of truth, beauty and goodness. The harmony of these values in a crystallised form appears to be what we usually understand by 'culture'. As human value, culture is something which is to be achieved by conscious, deliberate effort, by the self-cultivation of the individual. The culture of the individual is dependent upon the culture of the whole society to which the group or class belongs.[1]

Normally a scholar is regarded as a man of culture. Similarly a musician, a painter or a priest—each one is regarded as a man of culture. But culture as such comprehends all the disciplines or all human achievements in one whole where each has its own contribution. Proficiency in any one of human efforts does not constitute culture, because the culture of an individual cannot be isolated from that of the group, and the culture of the group cannot be isolated from that of the whole society. Culture is several cultural activities of several human beings—all taken into account at once. It is only by "an overlapping and sharing of interests, by participation and mutual appreciation, that the cohesion necessary for culture can obtain."[2]

Religion can be said to be rooted in the culture of a society in so far as a religion requires "not only a body of priests who know what they are doing, but a body of worshippers who know what is being done."[3] It will be seen that the cultural outlook of a society gives rise to one form of religion, and that of another, another form of religion and so on. If religious ideas and sentiments are overdone, then there may be a disintegration of culture. Again, if there is too much of cultural specialisation in one specific aspect, then religion may vanish.

In short, culture is what makes life worth living and religion only adds to it a specific colour which makes life meaningful. 'Spiritualism' is this specific colour. The phenomenon of culture is characterized by its inherent dynamism, its growth, its manifestation in the various aspects of human and social life. The growth is from the gross empirical to the refined trans-empirical. If the culture of a man is confined to gross empirical objects of Nature, then it is sheer pragmatism. It may, however, be rooted in pragmatism in its initial stage; but through stages of gradual development, as man is more and more refined in his pursuit of values, in his *looking through* the objects of Nature (and not just *looking at*) in his realisation of a higher purpose behind, culture steps into teleology. Thus from gross pragmatism to refined teleology is the development of culture through various stages of which religion is at the top with its intrinsic value known as 'spiritualism', where truth, beauty and goodness exist in perfect harmony with one another, and this is the conscious aim of mankind in his religious pursuit in and through the cultural environment.

Social values and religious values constitute the two aspects of human culture. The distinction, however, is lost when man attains the highest stage of culture. The value which shines at this stage and is ever-radiating is the human value or humanism which comprehends all the three fundamental values and also each one of the derivative values belonging to the domain of society or of religion. Culture requires the need of self-preparation by a feeling of want, an impulse which perpetually drives the man forward till he is consciously aware of the existence of *something beyond* and qualifies himself by a disciplined progress for the realization of this *something beyond* within himself. It is also the cultural outlook of man which provides an organisation of the individual and collective life, a framework of personal and social discipline and conduct, of mental, moral and vital development by which man moves on into new horizons of expectations for the fulfilment of his conscious endeavour to go beyond the initial limits of Nature.

Religion may thus be considered as the "religious culture" of a particular society in a given period of time. The dimensions of such a religious culture are never fixed for ever; they change according to the human needs of refining the total cultural outlook. Religious culture, or in short, religion does not necessarily require any name, for example, Hinduism or Christianity or Islam and so on. It sets before itself no dogma, no limitation of caste or creed, no narrow path towards salvation. It is a continuously enlarging tradition of the teleological endeavour of mankind. As an immensely multi-dimensional provision for self-searching and self-building, religion has some right to speak for itself without adhering to any name by which it may be branded. Religion is, therefore, the cultural pilgrimage of mankind; nobody knows where and when the journey ends. It is the spark of humanity, a call to which man responds instantaneously to the cause of *truth, beauty* and *goodness* in spite of the lack of competence to locate the positive reality of these values.

The flavour of culture as such and also of religious culture is lost, if man is isolated. The essence lies in the principle of unity and harmony. The unity is not a mere idea, but an energising truth. The consciousness of this unity is what is unique in man. Whatever name is given to it, or whatever form it symbolises, the conscious effort of man to realise this principle of unity within himself is religion.

"The development of intelligence and physical power", says Rabindranath[5], "is equally necessary in animals and men for their purposes of living; but what is unique in man is the development of his consciousness, which gradually deepens and widens the realisation of his immortal being, the perfect, the eternal. It inspires those creations of his that reveal the divinity in him—which is humanity—in the varied manifestation of truth, goodness and beauty, in the freedom of activity which is not for his use but for his ultimate expression. The individual man must exist for Man the great, and must express him in disinterested works, in science and philosophy, in literature and arts, in service and worship. This is his religion, which is working in the heart of all his religions in various names and forms. He knows and uses this world where it is endless and thus attains greatness, but he realises his own truth where it is perfect and thus finds his fulfilment."

The essence of religion consists in man's awareness of his creative impulse, man's understanding of the Unity of Nature and in the greater unity of himself with Nature, the first stage of which is interaction between man and Nature, the second stage, between man and man, the third stage, between the inner man and the outer man. Nature has its own channel of information for our mind and physical relationship with our body. But we have a feeling of intimacy with nature when it satisfies our personality with manifestations that make our life rich and opens our vision to the harmony of forms, colours, sounds and movements. It is not the Nature which bears good testimony to the science; but it is nature "which lavishly displays its wealth of reality to our personal self having its own perpetual reaction upon human nature."[6] Similarly in the interaction between man and man, each one inspires and is inspired by a common endeavour by which each man is enriched and encouraged in his higher pursuits in wide perspectives. Thus when a man comes to himself and looks inward he realizes that on the surface of our being we have the changing phases of our experience, but in the depth there dwells the eternal spirit of unity which is manifested in all our actions and in all beauties of Nature. Beyond the curtain of personal choice, habits and superficial conventions, man comes out with the call of supreme sacrifice of his individual self and melts away into the service of mankind in general in relation to Nature. This realisation is the reward of religion which is free from the bondage of images, temples, scriptures, prophets or rituals and ceremonies.

But the question may be raised: How can there be a religion which has no rigid dogmas demanding belief of pain of eternal damnation, no theology? How can there be a religion without a church or a temple or a mosque, without a congregational system? Sri Aurobindo[7] has himself raised these questions and the answer which he offers is the following:

> The supreme truths are neither the rigid conclusions of logical reasoning, nor the affirmation of credal statement, but fruits of the soul's inner experience. There are no true or false religions. All religions are true in their own way and degree. The least important part of religion is its dogma. Only the religious spirit matters, not the theological credo. Each religion is one of the thousand paths to the one Eternal.

It is not possible, nor advisable either to arrange the details of all the accepted religions of the world in a hierarchy. All religions answer in different ways to the fundamental question of human existence. Some may be regarded as superior to others in the sense that they are in need of higher mental functions and rigid asceticism, or that some are richer in ideas and sentiments containing more concepts and fewer images. But however real the greater complexity and the higher ideality may be, they are not enough to place the corresponding religions in different classes. All are equally religions just as all living beings are equally alive. They respond to the same human needs, they play the same role, they depend upon the same causes.[8]

But still the question remains: Why do we prefer to give religion a prerogative of its own? What is its distinctive merit by virtue of which it requires a special study other than that of man and society?

To this question Huxley[9] would reply that a way of dealing with the problems of human existence would not be distinctively religious if it did not stem from or encourage a feeling of sacredness of the major elements in its view of the world, man and human life. Religion, he would say, is a social organ for dealing with the problem of human destiny. As such it involves a conception of the world within which this destiny is significant together with some mobilization of the emotional and creative forces of human personality in relation to the world thus conceived.

It will be seen that the reply given by Huxley presupposes the distinction between the sacred and the profane, and consequently the view of religion which he wants to advocate would consist of ritual acts in the presence of sacred objects. He seems to be under the influence of the idea that religious beliefs are the representations which express the nature of sacred things, and religious rites are the rules of conduct which prescribe how a man should behave in the presence of sacred things. The argument in favour of this distinction would be that if everything of this world were sacred, then sacredness would lose its meaning; the sacred would be good for nothing.

The distinction between the sacred and the profane is of course said to be deep-rooted in the minds of men. Actually, the distinction, if at all drawn, is one of degree and not of kind. Moreover, it depends upon the human attitude with sufficient maturity whether or not the distinction has really to be drawn in order to save religion from mere fancy. On the contrary, one is inclined to feel that the distinction itself is arbitrary and speaks of human inability to read sacredness into the things of Nature. Nothing in the world is sacred by itself as nothing in the world is profane by itself. Sacredness is not anything glued on to the things. It is just a projection of human mind upon the things for which there is no convincing argument.

Things or entities are customarily regarded as sacred because some phenomena of nature arouse the feeling of fear and consequently demand an attitude of respect from persons who succumb to this element of fear. They are treated with respect not because of anything intrinsic in them, but because of some imposing or terrifying character at which the persons feel themselves quite helpless. The so-called sacred things are thus symbolic of some personal deities behind them who are more harmful than beneficial, or whose beneficial character is not always available. Such an attitude, far from being reasonable, is almost derogatory to any healthy attitude towards religion.

After all, what is sacredness? It is something in an object which inspires man to his higher pursuits in a richer universe where he can rest in peace. Discomfort or uneasiness is the psychological factor which drives man in search for the sacred things of the world. But discomfort or uneasiness is nothing but the psychological inability to find out unity and harmony in the objects of Nature. And once harmony is discovered, we can hasten to say that the harmonious thing itself is sacred. The principle of unity and harmony is the real criterion of sacredness and it only requires a man to have a vision to which it will be revealed. A man lacking in such a vision tends to characterise things as profane and engages himself in the so-called sacred things. This is a sort of escapism and has to be condemned. The terms themselves are unfortunate in so far as they are not rooted in the creative imagination of man. To a common man without a vision, a tree is just useful because it gives him a shade where he can take shelter in the scorching rays of the sun. But to a man with vision, a tree has its inner harmony which is manifested in its branches; it has its inner movement of life in *truth*, because its existence is undeniable; in its *beauty*, because it catches the interest, attention and concentration of the man; in its *goodness*, because it is expected to continue without disturbing anything else in Nature, and at the same time rendering unrewarded service to others.

Religion is basically a *human endeavour* of quest and conquest. The same is true of Science. But Science can only organize into well-ordered rational concepts the facts which man knows and understands. Religion, on the other hand, is the conquest of the march of life where the identity between the inner life of man and his outer life focussed on nature is established in and through the unifying principle of love, sympathy and wisdom which is much higher than knowledge and intellection. Science claims progress in human civilization. So also does Religion. The claim of a scientist ends in giving us a theoretical picture of the world. Science tells us what life is by theoretically analysing the anatomy of a living organism. But Religion teaches us how life is to be lived. External comforts of living offered by the scientist are of no use in respect of the inner peace of mind which is the product of religious lessons, the triumph of humanity. A rose gives us more delight than a piece of gold.

So the prerogative of religion can be said to consist not in the feeling of sacredness, but rather in the feeling of the harmony of self-adjusting interrelationship with Nature as a whole, which it is impossible either to analyse with the help of theoretical concepts or to practise with success through the accepted rituals and ceremonies.

It is only by regarding religion in this angle that we can hope to see its real significance. Durkheim has seen this point when he says that religious forces are human forces.[10] If we do too much of rituals and ceremonies, then there is the danger of their being purely manual operations which would result in a mechanical process where humanity is likely to disappear.

The essence of religion consists in the pure truth of love and goodness which we need not wait to learn from the theologians. It is within us and we only need to close our eyes to be able to see. "In the night we stumble over things and become acutely conscious of their individual separateness. But the day reveals the greater unity which embraces them. The man whose inner vision is bathed in an illumination of his consciousness at once realizes the spiritual unity reigning supreme over all differences. His mind no longer awkwardly stumbles over individual facts of separateness in the human world, accepting them as final. He realizes that peace is in the inner harmony which dwells in truth and not in any outer adjustments. He knows that beauty carries an eternal assurance of our spiritual relationship to reality, which waits for its perfection in the response of our love."[11]

It is now clear that heterogeneity or superficial separateness between things is the root cause of our blind distinction between the sacred and the profane. In reality, there is only homogeneity exhibiting the unity and harmony of things which requires the proper vision to realize. Any religion based on such a superficial distinction itself is superficial and is thus condemned.

Durkheim[12] maintains that the circle of sacred objects cannot be determined once for all; its extent varies infinitely according to the different religions. To this we like to add that everything is sacred from the point of view of its intrinsic harmony of its various components and its harmony with other things in Nature. Nature is harmony projected and exemplified and there is nothing in nature which can exist in total isolation. The magnanimity and dignity which are the special marks of sacred things are human projections and there is no reason why man chooses one and rejects other to locate the intended dignity as the essential requisites of any religious practice. There is no reason however to suppose that sacred things would lose their sacredness if there are no profane things, as there is no reason to suppose that man cannot be moral unless there are immoral persons. There is indeed no difficulty and no logical error to suppose that morality is an all-pervasive value and all human actions could be equally moral. The only thing to see is whether any given criterion is satisfied. And again there is no reason to hold that a criterion has to be formulated which by definition can only be partially satisfied.

Durkheim suggests that all religious faiths are rooted in man's social consciousness. In other words, society is the soul of religion. The totality of human actions through his intellectual and emotional awareness is what constitutes culture, and culture is the key-concept of our social consciousness. Every form of society has its own cultural overtone. Durkheim says that "society cannot make its influence felt unless it is in action and it is not in action unless the individuals who compose it are assembled together and act in common; ... it is before all else an active cooperation. Then it is action which dominates the religious life because of the mere fact that it is society which is its source."[13]

It has, however, been objected[14] that Durkheim's position leads to a circular reasoning because it seeks to treat religious patterns as a symbolic manifestation of society and at the same time to define the most fundamental aspect of society as a set of patterns of moral and religious sentiment.

The argument, it will be seen, has little force, since circularity, if there is any, is no fault. It is a sort of feed-back dimension which is said to relate society with religion, each being enriched by the other.

An antagonism between religion and culture may, however, be formulated in the following couple of ways:

(a) it may be argued that culture can be preserved, extended and developed only in the absence of any religious faith or dogma;

(b) it may be argued that the preservation and maintenance of religion need not reckon with the preservation and maintenance of culture. The products of culture might have to be rejected as frivolous obstruction to any spiritual life.

To discuss these points thoroughly one has to enter into a detailed study of the historical process as to how culture or religion develops and takes a definite shape. Without entering into such a stupendous task, it may be argued back that neither culture, nor religion is something which we already possess as finished products of our society. It is something which is always in progress assuming new and new dimensions; it is something towards which we strive. The most fundamental point of importance is that we can see a religion as the whole way of life of the people, from birth to the grave and that way of life is also its culture.[15]

The possibility of such an antagonism cannot, however, be ruled out very easily. But it can be maintained that it is not always necessary to judge a product of art by religious standards or to judge a religion by artistic standards. A particular religious faith may fall into decay or a particular cultural pattern may disintegrate. But society does not accept any vacuum. The decadence is soon filled up by a substitute, expectedly better and more refined. Rather it is the very nature both of religion and of culture that it grows on through alternative stages of relative decadence and refinement. Man cannot afford to remain indifferent either to culture or to religion. Aesthetic or cultural sensitivity must always be extended to spiritual realization and conversely.

Such a danger arising out of this possible antagonism has also been foreseen by Rabindranath. He emphatically adds that religion is basically the humanity of our God which can never fall into total decay. The decadence, if at all, may be seen to consist in the specific interpretation of this fundamental truth. The religious faculty is our luminous imagination which in its higher stage is unique to man. It offers us that vision of comprehensiveness which for the necessity of biological or physical survival is superfluous.

There are different levels of human mind as there are different faculties of human consciousness. But the field of vision "which is open to our reasoning and intellectual faculties becomes widened when emotions are brought into play. With moral discriminations added to them, the field is widened further. And once our spiritual insight lies open, infinitude becomes the limit. That which we see with our mind's eyes gives us more satisfaction. The human face attracts us more than a pretty flower. In addition to the harmony of form and features, the face displays the light of consciousness, a play of intelligence and a grace of emotional expression which make a simultaneous impact on our sense-perceptions, our intellect and our emotions. Such an appeal cannot get easily exhausted."[16]

Regarding the question of the extension of aesthetic sensitivity to spiritual perception, the poet unambiguously says that Beauty reveals God's majesty in the midst of this creation. Goodness does the same in the conduct of human living. "Goodness shows beauty not so much as a thing to be perceived or understood. The beauty of goodness is a thing of much wider and deeper significance—it endows man with Godliness. It is because of its intimate nearness that we do not always notice goodness as beauty. When we do realize this, our whole being overflows with happiness like a river in flood; we come to know then that nothing in the world can be more beautiful."[17]

The poet concludes that in the union of the Good and the Beautiful is true perfection. Whenever our mind can find its repose, it is Truth. Where the true is indubitably true to me, it is like love, it is like joy. Understood in this way, the realization of truth and the realization of beauty become one and the same thing. This is the underlying idea of all cultural patterns.

What is meant by 'culture' is and always should be religiously inclined and what is 'religion' must always have a cultural foundation. A superficial cleavage between the two appears to be a product of the distorted view of humanity itself. Any religion gives a meaning to life, provides the framework for a culture and protects humanity from boredom and despair. It does not and should not aim at a passive awareness of dead facts; its aim is to '*elicit and fortify whatever creative impulse a man may possess*.' It is always a human tendency and it never represents a strictly definable body of doctrines for us to follow without conviction. Religion is the liberation of the creative impulse in man and not the introduction of new and new forms of authority. And this creativity of human impulse is the essence of culture which finds its spontaneous expression in a variety of art forms.

II

Let us try to understand the essence of all religions by means of a possible value-free examination of their manifestation in human life and society. Incidentally we shall try to work out an ontology of religious consciousness which may be said to constitute the essence of religion. The human mind can be known through the ways in which it experiences reality and reacts upon it; similarly the essence of all religions can be understood through a study of the major items of religious situations and the manifestations of religious faith.

It is not advisable, however, to go through the details of the history of all existing religions, to analyse and explain the groups of the so-called religious phenomena, idolatry, nature worship—sacred stones, trees and animals, the worship of men, of Gods and Goddesses, magic and divination, sacrifice and prayer, doctrines, mythology, dogmas, philosophies, ethics and art and what not. A phenomenology of religion can mean no more than a systematic counterpart to the history of religion, a method of cross-cultural comparison of the constituent elements of religious beliefs and practices as opposed to their treatment in cultural isolation and chronological sequence.

Husserl's major interest is that all metaphysical presuppositions should be abandoned. We have to investigate what actually confronts us. Presuppositions are likely to prevent us from achieving our goal of direct analysis of essences or general structures. Thus our position is that of an impartial observer who is interested in excluding what does not belong to the universal essence. What at best we can do is to try to analyse the essentials of a religious situation in their totality within an intuitive grasp.

But there is a danger of constructing such a phenomenology of religion inasmuch as there exists no other religious reality than the faith of the religious believer. But if our view, though phenomenologically inclined, regarding the essentials of religion differs from the opinion and evaluation of the believer, then we are talking not of the essence, but of our own personal conviction which, in its turn, would be one form of religion exclusively our own. Thus a phenomenology of religion appears to be a suicidal attempt, religion being not merely a matter of concern, but of conviction of individual believers and their commitments.

It is here that we feel the necessity of including psychology; and a phenomenology of religion is expected to do justice to the basic facts of human consciousness.

Thus a phenomenology of religion should consist not merely of a description of the universal, essential features of religion as such, but also of a meticulous observation and analysis of the so-called religious reality as it has been admitted into the very life of the believer as a human being. The religious phenomenon is not anything by itself. It is a product of the interplay and interpenetration of subject and object in the very act of understanding. It is not produced by the subject alone, not substantiated, nor demonstrated either. It occupies the entire history of a man's emotional and vital activity, the core-content of the man himself. If the religious phenomenon can be studied in such a perspective, then of course, its essence cannot vary and the testimony of a believer cannot run contrary to such essentials of a religious situation, no matter how far his purely personal likes and dislikes may vary.

A phenomenology of religion is thus more than taxonomy; it is, as it were, a *theological therapy*. It can assist theology to organize facts, to penetrate into their significance, and to evaluate and use them for its doctrinal conclusions.

The task for the phenomenologists is to interpolate the religious experiences into one's life and understand them systematically; to reject the unfounded truth-claims of any doctrine which is accepted on blind impulses, to confront chaotic reality and testify to what has been understood as constituting the very essence. The most suitable analogy seems to be the phenomenon of love. To a man who does not love, nothing manifests. The lover's gaze to the beloved and the longing for love should indeed be there, but it should be all love, self-surrendering and melting into the beloved.

No religious phenomenon can be studied without reference to the primitive psychological structure of man, his basic psychology of imagination. Unless we have a direct access to the man in his totality we might have to fall back upon empty abstractions, or empirical hollowness, or even methodological embarrassments. To rely exclusively upon the outward manifestation of man's empirical beliefs and testimonies in a religious situation is a sort of philosophical sickness. Our experiences are regarded as relevant to the world because we have an unfounded belief in a God who in His self-contributed goodness warrants this relevance. But we have to overcome the dichotomy of God and the world, and discover a method of understanding, within reflection, our experiences which are directly related to the world and its underlying principles. This is a sort of transcendental turn and return based on a polarity of human attitudes.

In such a task the phenomenologist should be concerned with:

(a) *theoria*—the implications of aspects of religion;
(b) *logos*—the structure of different religious traditions; and

(c) *entelecheia*—the course of events in which the essence is realized by its manifestations. The course of events in religious contexts appears to follow a law of challenge and response. "Each relapse seems to evoke in religious people a strong desire for and an attempt at restoring religion. Actually this effort results in a rising of the religious level. The phenomenology of religion is man's inseparable companion. It is an invincible, creative and self-generating force."[18]

Theologians are usually open to the criticism that they cannot properly understand the significance of a religious tradition to which they are not personally committed. But the phenomenologists have a wiser course of approach. They are interested to ensure a complete and comprehensive understanding of religious beliefs and practices of man in general. They suspend all value-judgements which more often than not stand in the way of a full and sympathetic understanding of a religious situation.

The outstanding obstacle to any sympathetic understanding of religion is the belief in the existence of God. Without entering into the fundamental question "Can God know that He is God?" let us try to examine the merits of the so-called proofs for the existence of God.

Let us turn back for a while to Russell[19] who for his well-known open-mindedness could afford not to be a Christian. He does not believe in God and in immortality. He also does not think that Christ was the best and wisest of men, although he grants Him a very high degree of moral goodness.

But no more of this at the moment. Russell challenges the so-called proofs and finally throws them away as being unsatisfactory in every possible sense.

(a) It is argued that everything we see in this world has a cause and as we go back in the chain of causes we must come to a First Cause and to that we give the name 'God'.

To this Russell replies that the argument does not carry much weight because philosophers and scientists do not go after causes. Moreover, that there must be a first cause of all things cannot have any validity. If everything must have a cause, then God also must have a cause. If there can be anything without a cause, then everything could be without a cause. 'There is no reason why the world could not have come into being without a cause; nor, on the other hand, is there any reason to suppose that the world had a beginning at all. The idea that things must have a beginning is really due to the poverty of our imagination.'

(b) The natural law argument states that God had given a special privilege to the planets and they move uniformly around the Sun.

To this Russell replies that this is a simple and convenient explanation that saves us a lot of trouble of looking further for any better explanation. The law of gravitation apart, the point remains that most of what passes by the name of natural law are human conventions. The laws at which you arrive are statistical averages of just the sort that would emerge from chance. The question remains: Why did God issue just those natural laws and not others? If you say that He did it simply from His own good pleasure and without any reason, you then find that there is something which is not subject to law and so your train of natural law is interrupted. If there is any, then God Himself would be subject to a law and there is no advantage of introducing God as the intermediary.

(c) It is said that everything in the world is just so made that we can manage to live in the world and if the world was ever so little different we could not manage to live in it. This is the argument from design.

To this Russell humorously replies that human nose should be treated as being designed to fit the spectacles. He, however, refers to the theory of Darwin. It is not that the environment is made suitable for mankind. But mankind grew suitable to it and this is the basis of adaptation to the environment. There is no evidence of design in it.

(d) It is said that there would be no right or wrong unless God existed. The right is rewarded and the wrong punished by God. This is roughly the doctrine of divine justice and is put forth as the moral argument for the existence of God.

To this Russell replies that if God is all good, then right and wrong are independent of God's wish. Again, it would follow that God is a curious person who likes to punish human beings by forcing them make the wrong actions. He then becomes more undignified than many of the existing human beings, like one who wants to be satisfied by inflicting punishment on others. Or, we may say that the world is created by a Devil when God was asleep. To accept God as the source of divine justice is the same as the feeling that "there is a big brother who will look after you." That plays a very profound part in influencing people's desire for a belief in God, "but obviously falls a long way behind proving the existence of God."

The so-called ontological argument is perhaps too weak for Russell to refute. It is obvious that it involves the fallacy of begging the question. To presume perfection and then to ascribe existence is a clear sign of intellectual dishonesty.

If religion is said to be rooted in fear, fear of the unknown, of the mysterious, of defeat and of death, then Russell would readily reply that fear also is the parent of cruelty, and Religion and Cruelty would then go hand in hand. Incidentally Russell criticises the gross emotional factor involved in Christianity. He would not, however, hesitate to extend it to any form of existing religion. If the idea is that we should be all wicked if we did not hold to the Christian religion, then Russell would retort that people who held to it had been for the most part extremely wicked. "In the so-called ages of faith, when men really did believe the Christian religion in all its completeness there was the Inquisition, with its tortures; there were millions of unfortunate women burnt as witches; and there was every kind of cruelty practised upon all sorts of people in the name of religion."[20]

It may be mentioned in this connection that it is in the name of religion and morality that a very wide conspiracy was organised in U.S.A. to prevent Russell from accepting the Professorship of the City College of New York.

The output of Russell's polemic leads us to two basic guidelines: the first one is, to quote M. Buber, the total "eclipse of god" and the second one is the total abolition of all blind dogmas, faiths and gross emotional commitments with too much of consequent selfishness.

Russell wants us to stand on our own feet and look fair and square at the world—its good facts, bad facts, its beauties and ugliness, to see the world and conquer it by our love and knowledge. To respect the physical world is foolish. It should be studied from the point of view of interaction between the physical nature and the human nature. There is no short-cut to good life, whether individual or social. Merely going to the church regularly or attending religious ceremonies does not make a man religious or good. A good and religious life has to be built up by knowledge, self-control and sympathy. It is sympathy, to quote K.C. Bhattacharyya,[21] which is not '*sympathy for*', but a '*sympathy with*'. The age-old antithesis of mind and matter as subject and object is more or less illusory. Again, the antithesis between things that can be affected by human desires (and ends) and things that cannot be so affected is also deceptive, since the line between the two is neither sharp nor immutable.

Religion is an attempt to overcome the numbers of antithesis and this is roughly what a phenomenology of religion aims at where the philosophy of nature coincides with the philosophy of value.

This has been worked out by Buber[22] in his 'I-Thou' encounter. He distinguishes between three spheres which build up man's religious consciousness:

First, our life with nature; secondly, our life with men, and thirdly, our life with intelligible forms.

In the first phase, creatures live and move over against us, but cannot come to us and when we address them as *Thou*, our words cling to the threshold of speech.

In the second phase, the relation is open and it is in the form of speech. We can give and accept the *Thou.*

In the third phase, the relation is clouded, yet it discloses itself. It does not use speech, yet begets it. We perceive no *Thou*, but nonetheless we feel we are addressed and we answer—forming, thinking, acting. In each Thou, we address the eternal Thou. "Even if the man to whom I say *Thou* is not aware of it in the midst of his experiences, yet relation may exist. For *Thou* is more than *It* realises. No deception penetrates here; here is the cradle of the Real Life." Buber continues: "This human being is not *He or She*, bounded from every other *He* and *She*, a specific point in space and time within the net of the world; nor is he a nature able to be experienced and described, a loose bundle of named qualities. But with no neighbour, and whole in himself, he is *Thou* and fills the heavens. This does not mean that nothing exists except himself. But all else lives in his light."

According to Buber, the present is not fugitive and transient, but continually present and enduring. The object is not duration, but cessation or suspension. 'True beings' are lived in the present, and the 'life of the object' is in the past. The 'I' emerges as a single element 'out of the primal experiences, out of the vital primal words *I-affecting-Thou* and *Thou-affecting-I*, only after they have been split asunder and the participle has been given eminence as the object.'

Through the *Thou*, a man becomes *I*. That which confronts him comes and disappears, and in this process the *I* is enriched, each time stronger than before. Religious consciousness is basically the consciousness of the unchanging, ever-enduring partner, dynamically rooted in human consciousness of a perpetual interrelationship with the other, and understood in this way the *I-Thou* relation may roughly be regarded as constituting the ontology of religious consciousness.

Like Rabindranath, Buber also takes up the example of a tree. He says: 'The tree is no impression, no play of my imagination, no value depending on my mood; but it is bodied over against me and has to do with me, as I with it—only in a different way.' The tree is no longer the *It*, but it becomes the *Thou*. The *I-Thou* relation involves the whole man. "The fundamental mark of the *I-Thou* relation", comments M.L. Diamond,[23] "is not the full blown mutuality of speech and answering speech, but the intuition on the part of man, of the full ontological dimension of the other."

The *I-Thou* encounter constitutes what may be treated as a man's religious mode of being. This is a sort of essential and organic partnership into which the Divine enters into the human. Buber[24] boldly declares that he fails to understand the events of the so-called divine revelation, that there is a divine content as such which pours itself into a human vessel. The actual revelation seems to signify to him 'the breaking of the eternal divine light into the human manifoldness.' He knows no other revelation than that of the meeting of the divine and the human in which the human takes part just as well as the divine. For Buber, God is only the God of history.

A phenomenology of religion thus openly denounces the phrases like 'my religion' or 'his religion' or phrases like 'foreign religion' or 'religion indigenous'; it is concerned with the essentials of 'being religious', a mode of human existence which responds to the religiousness of human consciousness, which belongs to the reflective level of consciousness.

The major claim in a phenomenology of religion can be traced to the 'autonomy of human existence' and 'human freedom'. The first will be seen to invariably lead on to the second.

Sartre[25] maintains that the law of being in the knowing subject is *to-be-conscious*. Consciousness is not a mode of particular knowledge which may be called an inner meaning or self-knowledge; it is the demension of transphenomenal being in the subject. All consciousness is positional since it transcends itself in order to reach an object and it exhausts itself in this same positing. The reflecting consciousness posits the consciousness reflected-on, as its object. And it is in the reflective level that the autonomy of man's existence is ensured. "Being is, Being is in-itself. Being is what it is." Being includes both *being in-itself* and *being-for-itself*, but the latter is the nihilation of the former. As contrasted with existence, Being is all-embracing and objective, rather than individual and subjective. Reflection is the attempt on the part of consciousness to become its own object.

Existence, according to Sartre, is concrete individual *being here and now*. Since there is no pre-established pattern for the human nature, each man makes his *essence* as he lives.[26] To this essence we choose to confine the term 'Being'.

The autonomy of human being is not all subjective. It is not by "turning back upon himself, but always by seeking beyond himself, an aim which is one of liberation and of some particular realization that man can realize himself as truly human.[27] Sartre adds that man is "all the time outside of himself. It is in projecting and losing himself beyond himself that he makes man to exist; on the other hand, it is by pursuing transcendent aims that he himself is able to exist. Since man is thus self-surpassing, and can grasp objects only in relation to his self-surpassing, he is himself the heart and centre of his transcendence."[28]

Man's religious mode of being can thus be regarded as having a two-directional aspect—(a) it is subjective in so far as it has an assimilative and abstractive direction (abstraction from the concrete sensuous experience of nature), and (b) it is objective in so far as it has a projective or creative direction (projection of human attitude manifesting a richer universe of unity and harmony). In religious consciousness what is purely personal is dropped and what emerges is the '*Heart Universal*'[29] which is the core-content of all religious truths, the truths of perpetual humanization of nature.*

Religion involves a constant dissociation from the purely empirical situation and in this act of dissociation the 'empirically other' is reinterpreted in a richer and higher dimension which is one of spiritualism, where the 'empirically other' is, not as such negated, but transformed and transmuted in a totality.

Corresponding to all forms of mental behaviour in their comprehensiveness is Freedom as reflection, which is self-evident and self-certifying. Freedom is the phenomenological *prius* of all that is 'intended' in Nature as a whole.

Religion thus is man's phenomenological dedication to nature. In his religious mode of being Man organically participates in nature which is the projection of his own intrinsic feeling of harmony. Rabindranath happens to be the first Indian phenomenologist who has visualized the 'humanity of our god' or 'Divinity of Man the Eternal'. "We must realize", he says, "not only the reasoning mind, but also the creative imagination, the love and wisdom that belong to the supreme person, whose spirit is over us all, love for whom comprehends love for all creatures and exceeds in depth and strength all other loves, leading to different endeavours and martyrdoms that have no other gain than the fulfilment of this love itself."[31]

The notion of transcendence advocated in such a phenomenology of religion is counter-Platonic in the sense that it is rather a case of downward transcendence and not upwards. Man first confronts nature as it is, then negates it, and then reconfronts nature with the principle of unity and harmony as projected among the objects of nature and as manifested in the process of confrontation-projection. The 'going away' from Nature once for all is a kind of transcendence which was interesting to Plato. But the kind of transcendence which consists in 'coming back' to Nature is what is important here. By this element of transcendence man

*The concept of *Heart Universal* together with the two-directional aspect will be discussed in connection with Music and Man in Chapter 4.

reorganizes nature in order that he attains the fullness of his own spiritual life, and others too are elevated to proper vision and disinterested but concerned action. Transcendence is just the measure of man's spirituality and freedom.[32] The spiritual man is above the natural man. But the spiritual man is rooted in, but not exhausted by the natural man and herein lies his 'religiousness' which is a shorthand expression of man's freedom and transcendence. Religion is a function of man expressed in unifying, remoulding and in this function man is *impersonally free*.

From this freedom emerges the *sanctity of man* which also constitutes one major aspect of his spirituality. Such a sanctity is always teleological and never pragmatic. In his eternal quest of self-fulfilment through nature, man is always struggling to get through higher and richer truths of this harmony, the gateways of which are freedom and transcendence. Freedom is not just the ability to choose between alternatives; it is what constitutes the essential mode of being suited for man's religious endeavours. It is a surrender of the individual self to the Universal self through love, sympathy, sacrifice and the knowledge of the Truth.

For an understanding of the religious mode of being as constituting the ontology of religious consciousness the key-concepts are the following:

(a) Man-nature encounter resulting in the humanization of nature; (b) man's potential transcendence with a spiritual commitment but at the same time naturally inclined, and (c) the total life of man inspired by love and guided by knowledge. All these elements together constitute man's freedom which has an understood reference to (b) above and incidental but necessary reference to (a) and (c). Man's freedom understood in this sense may be compared to the freedom of a bird which flies over into the blue sky, but turns back to Nature as its eternal abode of peace.

Nature is the basic datum of man's religious consciousness, but man does not bow down to Nature. Nature is humanized, but never personified. Man is the ultimate and irrefutable arbiter of values, and in the world of value Nature is only a part. "Nature in itself is neutral, neither good nor bad, deserving of neither admiration nor censure. It is for us to determine the good life, not for Nature—not even for Nature personified as God."[33]

The superfluous character of theoretical ethics can be shown very easily by referring to the case of the illness of the child.[34] Love makes the mother wish to cure her child, and science tells her how to do. Love alone fails to cure the child. All our actions spring directly from desire for an end together with knowledge of means. Though love and knowledge are both necessary, love is more fundamental for leading a good life because it leads human beings to seek knowledge in order to find out *how to benefit* those whom they love. Where inanimate objects are concerned, there is no question of *delight*, inasmuch as there is no sense in speaking that we love and feel benevolent towards a landscape or a piece of music. Love, at its fullest, is 'an indissoluble combination' of the two elements, delight and well-wishing. The religious way of life is life inspired by love and guided by knowledge. In all manners, good life includes an element of animal vitality, otherwise human life would become dull and drab. It should rather be directed against all kinds of religious despotism, and corruption in the name of religion. Civilization should be something added to and not substituted for such a life. "The ascetic saint and the detached sage fail in this respect to be complete human beings. A small number of them may enrich a community; but a world composed of them would die of boredom."[35]

By 'culture' then is meant the life of man's religious mode of being, the spiritual life of man which a man cannot live in isolation from others. Culture manifests itself in a community of human beings with a definite, but not static, framework of values which accommodates the habits, customs, language, beliefs organised by intrinsic feeling of love and knowledge, where it is the *sanctity* of human life which prevails as the predominant value.

By religion, on the other hand, is meant a more or less total organization of human life with an emphasis on *sanctity* as the guiding principle which is directed towards Nature as a whole, wherein Nature figures as the embodiment of human values with an ever-growing purpose of self-realization which consists in augmenting the dimension of Nature and man's life therein as characterised by an intrinsic attitude of self-transcendence which is the measure of man's spirituality and the resulting freedom.

Man is the poet of nature with tender patience fused in his vision of *truth, beauty* and *goodness*. Religion consists in the grasp of the fundamental truth that the order, the depth, the value of the world in its whole, the beauty of the world, on the one hand and on the other, graceful tenderness and the peace of life are all bound together. It reveals a higher truth that the universe exhibits a creativity with infinite freedom and a realm of forms with infinite possibilities. But this creativity and these forms taken together cannot achieve actuality apart from the "completed harmony" which, with due reservations, we may choose to call 'God'.

Religion expresses a happy acceptance of the world in the man-nature encounter and a delight in being alive in it. The sense of living in a hostile world is for ever rejected by the feeling of man's self-confidence which is intrinsic in him. Religion is always self-externalization without self-estrangement. This is another side of the cultural background of man which spontaneously expresses itself in various art forms, whether visual art or performing art.

Art can thus be said as the condensed and refined form of self-expression; it is the crystallised model of communication with man himself, and with Nature which in every art form is ultimately humanised. Art is both enfolding and unfolding of the richness of the spiritual values of man through any chosen medium. The uniqueness in the artistic creativity consists in the realised identity of man with his eternal search for realities higher than what his mere cognitive abilities can afford. An artist being faithful to his religious and cultural commitments creates a richer universe which is beyond the boundaries of his own social consciousness. The principle of universal value which we have seen in man's religious and cultural mode of being is spontaneously revealed in his artistic creation.

Works of creative art, visual or performing, are customarily described by professional theorists and critics with the help of free-floating phrases, and thus such works are endowed with a kind of incomprehensible dynamism. This, in turn, serves to promote among the more imaginative artists, enriched with a depth of vision beyond the sensible world, a feeling of being able to reach the gateways of the transcendent and the ineffable. Consequently, art becomes a religious, or more appropriately, a *spiritual surrogate.*

Every work of creative art can be compared to a 'hungry ocean' which gains advantage on the kingdom of the shore increasing store with loss and loss with store.[36] It is the life of the creative and reflective higher self. We have already suggested in the context of religion that phrases like 'my religion' or 'his religion' should be abandoned; similarly in art or in culture such phrases are devoid of any significance. There is nothing in art like 'my creation'; it is 'art creating itself through a self-conscious higher personality somehow located in a body having a spatio-temporal reference'. Similar is the case with 'culture'—the reference may be either to individuals or to communities, but the appeal is universal. Such is the higher life which we live in art, in culture and also in religion, perhaps the three in one. In each of these endeavours there is a transcendental turn and between the higher life which is a life of spirituality (enriched by sanctity) and the life gained through intuitive apprehension there is a very thin, transparent line of division. To the one side of this line belong the creative artists, the genuine religion-humanists or the truly culturists who have caught a glimpse of this spiritual life and have breathed the pure air of growing vitality; to the other side of the line belong the connoisseurs in the field of art, the priests in the field of religion, and the reformers in the field of culture. This is also the line which divides the empirical from the spiritual, the truths of the former being calculative and cognitive and those of the latter being intuitive and caught in a *felt-whole* which is infinitely potential.

Spiritualism does not mean here the belief that departed spirits communicate with and show themselves to men, especially at seances by means of spirit-rapping, handwriting etc. It means the unique realization of the unity of the individual man with the transcendental Universal Man, the Supreme Soul which creates the universe.

Rabindranath[37] says:

> Truth is in unity and therefore freedom is in its realization. The texts of our daily worship and meditation are for training our mind to overcome the barrier of separateness from the rest of existence and to realize *advaitam*, the Supreme Unity which is *anantam*, infinitude. It is philosophical wisdom, having its universal radiation in the popular mind in India, that inspires our prayer, our daily spiritual practices. It has its constant urging for us to go beyond the world of appearances, in which facts as facts are alien to us, like the mere sounds of foreign music; it speaks to us of an emancipation in the inner truth of all things, where the endless *Many* reveal the *One*.

Religious perception consists in the understanding of such spiritual freedom within oneself. As in the world of religious perception, so in the world of art, the Indian artists gain an unobstructed vision of unity, the incarnation of the real which is a joy for ever. The world as an art is the play of the Supreme Soul revealing itself in imageries of diverse form.

The greatness, or rather the uniqueness of Indian art, consists in the vision of soul in all things. Rabindranath regrets that the West may believe, in some cases, that human beings have a soul; but she hardly believes that there is a Universal Soul.

We need not go into details of this rather controversial issue here. The most important point in Indian Art is that it has its root in religious perception. The Indian saints sit in meditation to realize the fundamental spiritual truth, and the Indian artists have joined them in their artistic creations. No confusion should be made between *religion* and a particular religious *cult*. Religious perception is like a flowing river, growing and progressing towards the endless ocean in a certain direction. And it is always on the basis of such perception that the Indian artists have tried in their respective ways to reveal their unique inward feelings of commitment making religious perceptions operative and meaningful in actual life. Such works of art, whether verbal, visual or performing, have always been highly valued and encouraged by a society which speaks of its cultural dimension.[38]

NOTES AND REFERENCES

1. T.S. Eliot, *Notes Towards the Definition of Culture*, p. 21.
2. *Op. cit.*, p. 24.
3. *Op. cit.*
4. The term is borrowed from *The Foundations of Indian Culture* by Sri Aurobindo.
5. *The Religion of Man*, p. 11.
6. *Op. cit.*, p. 12
7. *The Foundations of Indian Culture.*
8. The idea is borrowed from *The Elementary Forms of Religious Life*—E. Durkheim.
9. J. Huxley, *Religion without Revelation.*
10. E. Durkheim, *The Social Foundation of Religion* (a paper incorporated in the anthology entitled *Sociology of Religion,* edited by R. Robertson).
11. Rabindranath Tagore, *The Religion of Man*, p. 67.
12. *The Social Foundation of Religion.*
13. *Ibid.*
14. T. Parsons, *Religion and the Problem of Meaning*, a paper incorporated in the anthology entitled *Sociology of Religion.*
15. The antagonism and the reply are both suggested by T.S. Eliot in his monograph entitled *Notes Towards the Definition of Culture.*
16. *Rabindranath on Art and Aesthetics*, pp. 4-5.
17. *Rabindranath on Art and Aesthetics*, p. 6.
18. This is the view of C.J. Bleeker—*The Sacred Bridge*, borrowed from *Comparative Religion—A History* by E.J. Sharpe, p. 237.
19. *Why I am not a Christian.*
20. *Ibid.*, p. 15.
21. *Studies in Philosophy*, Vols. I and II (edited by Prof. Gopinath Bhattacharya).
22. M. Buber, *I and Thou.*
23. Paper on 'Dialogue and Theology' as incorporated in *The Philosophy of M. Buber* edited by A. Schilpp in the series 'The Library of Living Philosophers'.
24. The philosopher replies, *op. cit.*, p. 698.
25. *Being and Nothingness.*
26. The distinction between 'existence' and 'being' is not pursued here for the sake of relevance. The terms are here taken to be almost co-extensive but non-linear because of the religious context where the emphasis is more on humanism than either on being or on existence.
27. *Existentialism and Humanism*, p. 56.

28. *Ibid.*, p. 55.
29. The term is borrowed from K.C. Bhattacharya—*Studies in Philosophy*: paper on 'The Concept of Rasa'. This concept will be discussed in details in the sequel.
30. The analysis of the notion of freedom from the phenomenological point of view is borrowed from Prof. Kalidas Bhattacharya—*Nature and Freedom*; Published in the proceedings of the Conference held at Visva-Bharati under the auspices of the International Metaphysical Society.
31. *The Religion of Man*, p. 15.
32. The idea is borrowed from Prof. Kalidas Bhattacharya on *Religion—What It Exactly Means*.
33. B. Russell, *Why I am not a Christian*, p. 44.
34. The example is borrowed from Russell.
35. B. Russell, *Why I am not a Christian.*
36. The idea is borrowed from Shakespeare's 'Time and Love'.
37. *The Religion of Man*, pp. 115-116.
38. This chapter is a revised version of an earlier draft of my paper published in *Visva-Bharati Journal of Philosophy*, February 1984.

CHAPTER 2

VISUAL ART AND PERFORMING ART

I

The world of art falls into three major groups: (a) Verbal (literature including prose, poetry and plays), (b) Visual (painting, sculpture and architecture) and (c) Performing (music, dance and drama). In this chapter we propose to discuss (b) and (c), more particularly (c), which would enable us to enter into a further study of Indian music and its spiritual background. Incidentally, the issue of verbal art would be discussed.

The arts are roughly divided into (a) *arts in space* which refer to visual arts and are also sometimes described as spatial arts because they occupy space with length and breadth, a two-dimensional phenomenon, generally a canvas, a wall or even a portion of land for a piece of architecture or sculpture. The artists successfully introduce an effective appeal of the third dimension, namely depth, and also to an extent the fourth dimension, namely motion. Here the objects of art appear to be moving, or some impression of dynamism is introduced; (b) *arts in time* which refer to music which lasts only as long as it is produced, each note in the musical art lasting for a measured period of time as necessitated by the total aesthetic appeal; and (c) *arts in space and time* which refer to dance and theatre which exist in space and continue for a definite period of time. The situation is rather difficult as regards literature or verbal art. It can be said with due reservation that it exists in space, since articulated language in pages occupies durability wherein permanence is ensured.

All great works of visual art, as we have already seen, proceed from an intuitive glimpse of some truths of human life inclined towards something higher than its gross empirical level, something which is more significant than the mere individuality. The chief characteristic of Indian art lies in its unique task to disclose something of the Infinite, the Supreme soul through its living finite symbols. This something cannot be completely described in so far as it is revealed or in some way suggested to the soul's intrinsic understanding or "to its devotion or at the very least to a spiritually or religiously aesthetic emotion. When this hieratic art comes down from these altitudes to the intermediate worlds behind ours, to the lesser godheads or genii, it still carries into them some power or some hint from above. And when it comes quite down to the material world and the life of man and the things of external Nature, it does not altogether get rid of the greater vision, the hieratic stamp, the spiritual seeing, and in most good work—except in moments of relaxation and a humorous or vivid play with the obvious—there is always something more in which the seeing presentation of life floats as in an immaterial atmosphere. Life is seen in the self or in some suggestion of the infinite or of something beyond or there is at least a touch and influence of these which helps to shape the presentation. It is not that all Indian work realises this ideal..., but it is the best and the most characteristic influence and execution which gives its tone to an art and by which we must judge. Indian art in fact is identical in its spiritual aim and principle with the rest of Indian culture."[1]

Ananda K. Coomaraswamy[2] is of opinion that *to think for oneself* is always *to think of oneself.* This he calls 'freethought' which is the natural expression of a humanistic philosophy. 'Freethought' may be said to be a free union of 'free contemplation' and 'free enjoyment' which is a sublime joy of the human soul in his artistic creativity. The inspiration which the artist may incidentally derive from the immense wealth of Nature elevates the very being of the artist to super-conscious and supra-individual levels.[3] The inspiration, according to Sri Aurobindo, is the emotion of the spirit of which the mental equivalents are subordinate in helping the act of transmission in colour and shape.

The elements of form, colour, line, design etc., are only the physical means of artistic creativity in cases of visual art. In using them, says Sri Aurobindo, the man behind is not bound to imitation of Nature. He has to make the form and everything else significant to his spiritual vision. The artist has full freedom in making any symbolic variation, because true to his own vision he is creating or expressing himself, the unity of the thing and his being. The colour, line etc., are his last, and not the first, preoccupation because they have already taken a spiritual form in his intrinsic capacity to invite Nature within his own being. Sri Aurobindo[4] clarifies this point with the help of an example. The artist has not to re-create the face and body of *the Buddha* or some one passion or incident of his life. He has to create *the calm* of *Nirvāna,* through a figure of *the Buddha.* When it is some human passion or incident, the artist has to create. "It is not that alone, but also something else in the soul to which it points or from which it starts or some power behind the action that has to enter into the spirit of his design and is often really the main thing. And through the eye that looks on his work he has to appeal not merely to an excitement of the outward soul, but to the inner self, *antarātman*." Sri Aurobindo hastens to add: "One may well say that beyond the ordinary cultivation of the aesthetic instinct necessary to all artistic appreciation there is a spiritual insight or culture needed if we are to enter into the whole meaning of Indian artistic creation, otherwise we get only at the surface of external things or at the most at things just below the surface. It is an intuitive and spiritual art and must be seen with the intuitive and spiritual eye." To this we propose to add that the same is true regarding Indian Music.

Every work of Indian art, whether visual or performing, rests on the interlocking of the visible and the invisible with a veil as transparent as possible so that an access to the invisible, the Infinite is not impossible, however immensely difficult it may be though.

A comparative study of the Indian and Western view on art in general might not be out of context here. Once more we turn back on the interpretation given by Sri Aurobindo.

The western mind, according to Sri Aurobindo, is arrested and attracted by the form. It lingers on it and cannot get away from its charm, loves it for its own beauty and emphasises the emotional-intellectual suggestions that arise from it most obviously. To the western mind *form* creates the *spirit,* and the *spirit* depends for its existence and for everything it has to say on the *form.* The Indian attitude is at the opposite pole. To the Indian mind, *form* does not exist except as a creation of the *spirit,* and draws all its meaning and value from the *spirit.* "Every line, arrangement of mass, colour, shape, posture, every physical suggestion, however many, crowded, opulent they may be, is first and last a suggestion, a hint, very often a symbol which is in its main function a support for a spiritual emotion, idea, image that again goes beyond itself to the less definable, but more powerfully sensible reality of the spirit which has excited these movements in the aesthetic mind and passed through them into significant shapes."[5]

In the Indian context of visual art, it is rather a controversial issue whether Moghul art can really be classified under genuine works of Indian art, because, according to the Experts, Moghul art embodies the intermixture of various influences from a large number of foreign cultures; it might itself be treated as foreign to Indian soil. Barrett and Gray in the introduction of their book entitled *Treasures of Asia—Indian Painting* have observed:

> By the fifteenth century, especially in the provinces of Gujarat and Bengal, a new style of architecture had evolved to which the native contribution was so large and vital that we are entitled to speak not of Muslim art in India but of Indian art for the Muslim patron..... Utilized at the Mughal and provincial Muslim Courts for portraiture, hunting and zenana scenes, it was transported during these troubled times (*perhaps the reference is to the reign of Aurangzeb*) to the comparative security of Panjab Hills. Now close to the Indian conception of picture-making, it was immediately accessible to the Hill artist and swiftly supplanted the older style. A vehicle in its new environment for a tender and romantic statement of the Krishna legend, it sustained the Indian vision for a further two generations.*

We propose not to enter into a detailed study of Moghul art at this stage. Whatever is said of Indian art applies to all the different stages of history right from the ages of Mohenjo-daro and Harappa, covering the Aryans and the Dravidians, down to the modern period travelling through the diverse paths of Hinduism, Buddhism, Jainism, Saivism, Vaisnavism and all other cultural frameworks which are rooted into the soil of India. The art of India will eternally survive, because the artists are the sons of the soil and in their art sing the celestial song of joy in living the life of a real human being in the fullness of its existence.

In his comparative study with the western art, Sri Aurobindo makes a reference to a very significant and illuminating point. With due humility, he argues that crowded art-galleries or over-pictured walls are perhaps the right conditions for display of western visual art. In contrast, Indian art (whether painting or temples, sculptures, palaces) can be seen away on the mountains or at the remotest corners of a village where the undisputed spiritual suggestions of art with their treasured secrecy have the proper appeal to a mind when the soul is at leisure from life. The great works of Indian art do not and by nature cannot reveal the secrecy of its spiritual dimension to one who has only an aesthetic curiosity, but no commitment. Exceptions granted; but this is an indication, according to Sri Aurobindo, of the utmost value pointing to the nature of the appeal in Indian art, and the right way and mood for looking at and interpreting its creations. Once again we add that the same is true of Indian music to which we shall shortly come.

Indian art may be criticised by the western scholars as empty

*Italics within brackets mine.

metaphysical pursuits, because to them it emphasises what is a matter of sheer speculation approaching the height of meaningless absurdities. Such a criticism is not only unfortunate, but unfair. The Supreme Soul or the Cosmic Spirit or the Infinite (whatever terminology one prefers) stands for the surplus in human potentials. In Indian context, Man perpetually tries to convince himself against his natural inclinations to the so-called paradox that he *is* not simply what he *appears* to others; but he is something greater. He has a vision of a Being who exceeds him in truth and with whom he has his intimate kinship.

It may be argued that Indian art introduces in our way of life a certain depth of imagination which "has its danger in aberrations that are intellectually blind, morally reprehensible and aesthetically repellent."[6] But these are defective and faulty attitudes towards Indian art as such.

These wrong answers distort the intrinsic truth of Man and such truth has to be judged by the standard of human perfection and not by some "arbitrary injunction that refuses to be confirmed by the tribunal of the human conscience."[7]

To the so-called Western criticism of *being empty metaphysical*, Rabindranath gives us a very convincing example from our empirical life. He refers to the mother's experience of her child-birth. He argues that a mother can and does realise the mystery of life of the child in her womb more intimately than man can ever do! She has directly felt the deep stir of life within her own being. This is not done through any process of intellectual argumentation; but this is possible only through the illumination of her own feeling, a feeling which is uniquely her own. So the same idea which is a mere abstraction or mere empty, idle speculation to one whose sense of reality is limited becomes luminously and concretely real to another whose sensibility has a much wider and deeper range. Similarly the western critic suffers from gross limitation of his sense of reality. The spiritual dimension of Indian art is so real to Indian mind that to deny it is to deny the sunlight in the sky. Rabindranath draws a final curtain to any type of western criticism of Indian art which in his opinion is based on a distorted view of Indian philosophy in general and philosophy of the Vedas and the Upanishads in particular. He argues that "as the illumination of man's *personality* throws its light upon a wider space penetrating into hidden corners, the world of art also crosses its frontiers and extends its boundaries into unexplored regions. Thus art is signalising man's conquest of the world by its symbols of beauty, springing up in spots which were barren of all voice and colours. It is supplying man with his banners, under which he marches to fight against the inane and inert, proving his living claims far and wide in God's creation."[8]

Indian art has its birth when there is a felt element of the superfluous in our hearts' spiritual relationship with Nature. According to Rabindranath, Indian art builds for its abode a paradise where only those impulses and feelings are needed that have transcended the earth's mortality. Again we add that the same is true whether the art is visual or performing, whether it is a poem or a painting or a piece of music.

It is normally accepted that great art is an unconscious creation. It would be a mistake to say that the artist *wants* to discover or uncover, create and communicate beauty, though it is granted that in the artistic work the elements of discovery, creation and communication are very much present. Every work of art is spontaneous creation, and for this reason it is always occasional. Art is not meant for creation of beauty, but beauty is always present in a work of art because it grows out of proportion, harmony and depth. Nature produces a vibration in the *will* of man, and not merely in his *cognition* which transforms into a spiritual *contemplation* and a resultant *enjoyment*. And what emerges is a work of art.

Let us try to understand the beauty of a living man, of his portrait and of his statue. In all these three cases what is discernible is the supremacy of the *will* over feeling and cognition. In the first case it is the Nature's will or the cosmic will, the Supreme Spiritual Will of the so-ealled God, the Creator or *Brahmã* spontaneously choosing the medium and the form; in the second and the third case, it is the human will spiritually inclined in his choice of the medium and form. In the two latter cases there is indeed no imitation; all the time man as an artist is engrossed in his own creation, the connecting link is the *will* working in the background in each case in its own unique, unpredictable way. What is of primary importance in each case is the spiritual significance of the will, whether Supreme will or human will, and the spirituality of the significance is exhibited by perfect proportion and harmony and unity wherein dwells beauty. Of the three varieties of art mentioned, the first one customarily belongs to natural beauty or divine creation, and the second together with the third belong to artistic beauty or human creation. In all these cases there is a progressive approach from material perception to reflection and spiritual understanding, revealing itself in a sense of unity and identity of the creator artist and the elements involved, along with the added element of involvement as such.

Visual arts are characterized chiefly as the rhythmic creations of line and structure. Rabindranath would say that his pictures are only versification in lines. If they can claim any recognition it must be for some rhythmic significance of form which is ultimate. It is not meant for any interpretation of *idea* or a representation of any *fact*. The ultimate significance of form is nothing but its spiritual appeal which is the spontaneous outcome of the human will in reflection of the basic unity with the Supreme soul from within. In the introduction of his *Chitralipi* Rabindranath says:

> The world of sound is a tiny bubble in the silence of the infinite. The universe has its only language of feature, it talks in the voice of pictures and dance. Every object in this world proclaims, in the dumb signal of lines and colours, the fact that it is not a mere logical abstraction or a mere thing of use, but it is unique in itself, it carries the miracle of its existence.

Any work of Indian art wants not to be beautiful; it only wants to live. And its life is ensured by its dynamism in rhythm and form, its spiritual depth.

About the overwhelming supremacy of Indian visual art Havell[9] says:

> Twenty-four years ago I was sent to India in order to instruct Indians in art, and having instructed them and as well as myself, to the best of my abilities, I returned amazed at the insularity of Anglo-Saxon mentality which has taken a century to discover that we have more to learn from India than India has to learn from Europe.

This firmly corroborates the view of the Indian art as we have developed earlier in connection with the observations of Sri Aurobindo and Rabindranath. There cannot be any doubt that Havell was impressed by the deep spiritual dimension of Indian paintings and sculpture, a unique and everlasting feature in the history of visual art. In the sequel we shall see almost the same reaction as regards Indian music which is equally spiritually dominated.

Unlike Sri Aurobindo, Rabindranath has a privileged position in any discussion on Art because he himself is a poet, a painter and a musician, three-in-one. But being true to the Indian way of life, to the fundamental genesis of Indian philosophy, both of them have spoken emphatically, and of course correctly, about the role of spirit in artistic creations. Whether belonging to the West or to East, any serious thinker would readily acknowledge that the greatness in any work of genuine art consists in a spiritual activity. It is a spiritual dictum so much so that when art attains the height of perfection, it goes beyond its medium and the artist finds himself realising that his instruments are not properly adequate to the spirit of what he seems to have tried to say.

The intrinsic principle which an artist has to follow, rather unknowingly, can be analysed into three elements:

(a) the element of *personality*: Every artist, as a creator, has something in him, some inner vision which *demands* expression through any medium.

(b) the element of *style*: Every artist, as a son of his time, is impelled to express the *spirit of the age* designed by the specific socio-cultural orientation of the particular period to which he belongs.

(c) the *essence* of art: Every artist, as a servant of art and master of his unique vision, has to uphold the *cause of art* (art regarded as *endotelic*) which leaves a permanent stamp in all ages and among all nationalities. By *endotelic* art is meant here self-objectification. *Autotelic* art means simply the skill in games and play, whereas *ectotelic* art means the utilitarian arts or skilled works like engineering, technology, craftsmanship, carpentry etc.

Kandinsky[10] has rightly drawn our attention to the important factor that a full understanding of the first two is necessary for the realisation of the third. The essence, or more appropriately the quintessence of art will remain for ever. He adds that time, far from diminishing its importance, increases it. "He who realises this will recognise that a rudely carved Indian column is an expression of the spirit that actuates any advance-guard work."[11] The greater the part played in any work of art by the elements of style and personality, the better will it be appreciated by the contemporary connoisseurs. But the artist in whose work the third element predominates is undoubtedly the greatest of artists. Sometimes centuries have to pass for a proper recognition of this third element. It is in the third element that spirituality in Indian art can be discerned.

Specialists in the field of art are concerned very much with 'style'; but the question, we fear, might lose its sharpness under the perspective of time. Some would prefer to say that style is always individual, because the style of any one person is not exactly the same as the style of any other person. Some others may say that style is the personality of the artist showing through medium, elements and organisation.

But the real fact which they ignore is that many people are alike in great many respects, and accordingly we have various styles—the Italian style, the French style, the Greek style, the Egyptian style and also the Indian style. Again we may say that we have classical style or romantic style or folk style and so on. This only shows that style may also be understood in historical perspectives or cultural perspectives.

What we propose to maintain is that in any work of visual art what is really individualistic is the technique of *how* things are manipulated or organised; the question of style, on the other hand, concerns the question: *why* are they so organised? And the answer can only be found in the personality of man which works in a couple of ways, centripetal and centrifugal. This can be best understood in the Indian context with the help of the observations of Rabindranath.[12]

> The Supreme Being is giving himself in his world and I am making it mine, like a poem which I realise by finding myself in it. If my own personality leaves the centre of my world, then in a moment it loses all its attributes. From this I know that my world exists in relation to me, and I know that it has been given to the personal *me* by a personal being. The process of the giving can be classified and generalised by science, but not the gift. For the gift is the soul unto the soul..... Therefore the one cry of the personal man has been to know the Supreme Person.

According to Rabindranath, man has been, from the beginning of the history, feeling the touch of personality in all creation and trying to give it names and forms breaking out in ceaseless flow in songs, pictures and poems. Personality in art is, therefore, a combination of a *centrifugal impulse* and a *centripetal force*.

Understood in this way, one can clearly see that the quintessence in Art, as we have mentioned as the third item of the three-fold requirements, cannot be understood in isolation from the first two. And there cannot be any work of Indian art where *only* the third item predominates. The distinctive feature of Indian art is that it is always a manifestation of all the three items together, the one inevitably leading on to the other, because all the three are very closely interwoven. In the continuity of its spiritual endeavour lies the best hope of Indian art for the future where time cannot destroy its greatness and magnificence because the spiritual fire in man is always at work in Art.

II

Before we enter into the details of performing art, let us introduce a few points on the 'form' of art which will be developed along as the discussion proceeds. By 'artistic form' is generally meant an enhanced spatio-temporal super-structure with a hidden *endotelic* treasure leading to a multi-dimensional aesthetic response and repose.

The question of 'form' in the works of art arises with the parallel question: By what principles does the artist transcend *nature* and enhance existential structure in the direction of greater intrinsic aesthetic interest? The answer to this question will naturally throw the needed light on the question: What is exactly meant by the *form* in Art?

This issue is vitally important and at the same time complicated to some extent. There is a large variety of opinion among the theorists regarding the definition of 'form' in art—and it is not unexpected either; we shall try to elicit some of the major points from the long debate among the theorists which might help us to understand what *form* means.

It may be said, to start with, that there are five fundamental principles to determine the *form* of any work of art. These are: harmony, balance, depth, development and centrality. Some theorists[13] have emphasised the *associates* and *derivatives* of these five major principles. These are: recurrence, similarity, gradation, variation, modulation, symmetry, contrast, opposition, equilibrium, rhythm, measure, dominance, climax, hierarchy and progression.[14]

These principles, determining the *form* of an artistic creation, apply to all forms of art, whether visual or performing or verbal, according as the case may be. It will suffice to mention that these principles and their derivatives are said to operate in two levels—presentational and representational. "In a painting there may be a harmony or balance between colours or shapes or lines. But there may also be a harmony or balance between suggested actions or attitudes or between represented personages within a scene or between the glint in the eye and the gesture of an arm of a single represented personage. The representational side of the painting may be as composed, as harmonised, as balanced, as are the lines or shapes or colours. Centrality and development may be similarly employed on the two levels.... As to development, it may appear merely on the presentational level as in the progressive unfolding of an abstract dance pattern or a pattern of musical sounds. But it may equally appear on the representational level in the progressive unfolding of a character, a course of action or an idea in a drama, an opera, or a novel."[15]

The passage is too clear and suggestive to require any further elaboration. On closer analysis it may appear that the principle of development, in a subtle sense, also applies to painting or sculpture, and not merely to art forms belonging to performing art. However, it must also be added that in so far as performing arts are concerned, the principle of development is the key-concept in contributing to the form of artistic creation, since the reference to time is dominant in performing arts.

In music, however, the artistic form can be said to consist in the whole body of the system of relations exhibiting a uniform pattern where inter-dimensional and intra-dimensional movements are exhibited. This point will be clear as we proceed.

Let us now pass on to a discussion of some fundamental characteristics of music as the chief work of art in the world of performing arts. It is said that music is the finest and purest of all arts. Why it is said so, is our main concern here, and we shall try not to turn our attention from this point.

Music is primarily divided into vocal and instrumental, and both deal with abstract sounds as heard. Both vocal and instrumental music were in vogue in the Vedic period. Vocal music was confined to the *chanting* of the *Sāma-mantras*. It is said that in the period of *Brāhmana* and *Saṃhitā*, the saints had a keen sense of music. They successfully tried to catch the musical element from natural sounds. The chanting is the earliest form of Indian music, and it is not to be confused with mere recitation. The *Sāma* chanting was usually accompanied by *Vinā* (lute) and *Dundubhi* (drum). The lute was considered to be a sacred instrument. The songs were meant in praise of several Deities. But behind the aspect of prayer, the appeal was to transcend one's own natural limitations and thus the element of spirituality could be found at the very root of Indian music, and it is said to be continued even today. It can even be said that spirituality in India first manifests in music.

The singers of the Vedic age were composers and performers at the same time. This is one of the chief characteristics of Indian music which gives it a unique dimension as distinguished from all other music forms of the world. To this point we shall again come in subsequent chapters. In this age it was not compulsory that everybody had to sing. Options were there to compose songs and once a song was composed by someone it was, in a sense, compulsory that he had to sing it. Dance, which is another item of the performing arts, was also practized at this age. If the saints can say that days and nights follow each other in a regular rhythmic manner like dancing, it is just one step forward to argue that for such saints dance was a serious art form and there must be some prescribed rules for it. When the Goddess *Vāk* was sent by Gods to dupe the *Gāndharvas* and fetch *Somarasa*, she (Vāk) started dancing and singing in order to please the *Gāndharvas.*[16] It may not be too impertinent to construct an argument that possibly Rabindranath in modern times was inspired by this episode in his compositions of dance-dramas. The content of the songs in this period belonged to *Ṛk-veda*, but the *Sāma* gave it a musical composition and a rendering in performance.

The discoveries of Indus-Valley civilization compel us to admit that practice of music did not start with the Vedic civilization, because such discoveries abound in relics of musical instruments and their use. The evidence of sculptures in the age of Indus-Valley civilization is a sufficient proof of the practice of both vocal and instrumental music and also of dance. But on such discoveries, no systematic theory can be constructed. We have to depend on Vedic civilization for a systematic account of the theory and dimension of Indian music.

In the Vedic period, roughly extending from 3000 B.C. to 600 A.D., some materials could be gathered particularly from the music of the *sāmagāna* on the basis of which we can derive in a rudimentary form a musical scale, the elements of *murchanā* (practizing a given scale changing the starting key-note), *tāla* or rhythm, and a vague and rather obscure system of notation. Since the style of *Sāmagāna* has almost disappeared, one cannot definitely say anything about the style of singing practized. But it is clear that music was mainly devotional and was practised on occasions of prayer or other forms of offerings to the Deities. The devotional character of the ancient Indian music proves beyond doubt the spiritual impulse of man out of which music flows and in course of time takes a concrete shape.

Sāmagāna, as a mode of chanting, is said to use three notes, namely, *udātta* (high-pitched tone), *anudātta* (low-pitched tone) and *svarita* (the middle one). These three notes may be said with ample reservation to constitute a musical scale, because some musicologists have argued that *udātta* corresponds to *rishava, anudātta* to *nishāda* and *svarita* to *sādjā* of our present day terminology in music. Gradually the songs of the Vedic age were composed on the basis of a fixed scale consisting of five, six or seven notes (as the case may be) and they were in a descending order as follows. The descending order is warranted by the intrinsic capacity and tendency of human voice.

Vedic notes (Vaidika)	*Present day notes (laukika)*
1. *Kruṣta (Udātta)*	1. *Pancama*
2. *Prathama*	2. *Madhyama*
3. *Dvitiya*	3. *Gāndhāra*
4. *Tritiya (Svarita)*	4. *Rishava*
5. *Caturtha*	5. *Sādjā*
6. *Mandra*	6. *Niṣāda*
7. *Atisvarya (Anudātta)*	7. *Dhaivata*

The *Sāmagāna* and its various forms are the rudiments of what is called *vaidika* music; at a later stage *laukika* music develops with the *gāndharvas* on the basis of their formalised and systematised notation system and is roughly called *deśi* music. The western *solfa* system of notation consisting of seven notes (*do, re, mi, fa, so, la, ti*) which was acknowledgedly discovered by *Guido D'Areezzo* (Tenth century) corresponds to the Indian present day musical scale of *sā, ri, gā, mā, pā, dhā, ni*. It should not be interpreted that the latter originated from the former. In all probability, the western musicologists and the Indian ones independently discovered the musical notes and the order of their arrangement in ascending scale. The order of the descending scale remains the same starting from the other end.

In two parallel lines the ancient music of India is said to develop—one in composing melodic patterns, whether simple or intricate on the basis of the selection and order of the notes, and the other in building the style and techniques of presentation keeping in view the form and content of some lyrical structures. The former is technically called the "*origin of Rāga system*", and the latter leads on to the discovery of the forms of musical compositions under the dominance of the style and technique of presentation. To the former belong the *Rāgas* or the melodic patterns like *Bhairavi, Yaman, Khāmāj, Bilāval, Āshāvari* etc., and to the latter belong the musical compositions like *Dhruva, Prabandha, Dhruvapada* or *Dhrupada, Kheyāl, Thumri, Tappā* etc.

It is mainly under the patronage of the Muslim Emperors of the mediaeval period that the ancient Indian music which was confined to forests or temples or villages was brought to court for the purpose of entertainment. But it must be added that whether in a temple or in a court, Indian classical music never lost its underlying spiritual dimension. All this applies to *Hindustāni music* or music practised in North India. In south India the music practised is termed '*Karnātika music*' which has not a much different story than the ancient music in India so far as its origin and development are concerned. But in the mediaeval period, it also took a turn and was systematised under a different fashion. In the classification of the melodic patterns, the chief guiding principle of *Hindustāni music* is said to be the '*Thāta*' system introduced by *Pandit Bhātkhande* and that of *Karnātika music* is the '*mela*' system introduced by *Pandit Venkatamākhin*. This is perhaps the most widely accepted view.

The system of classification apart, there is an immensely vast difference in the style of presentation of the two major schools of Indian classical music. The *tāla* system along with the specific percussion instruments meant for accompaniment are also widely different. Widely different are also the instruments used in the field of instrumental music, except perhaps the violin and the flute which happen to be accidentally common to both the schools. The case of *Veenā* is debatable because of the difference in the details of the structure of the instrument concerned.

Karnātika music, because of its rather over-emphasis on the mathematical calculation of notes and their sequences, loses much of the desired aesthetic-emotional appeal which is, on the other hand, very increasingly dominant in *Hindustāni music*. The excessive use of *gamakas* on a single note or on successive notes in undue fast pass-over, and the long time-span devoted to *gamakas* are perhaps responsible for the loss of the expected charm and the inherent spiritual depth characteristic of Indian music. The elements of proportion and balance required for creating the totality of aesthetic appeal in any given music form appear to be missing from *Karnātika* music. The reason is perhaps too much of intellection of art form than what is required. Thus *Hindolam* of *Karnātika* music fails to create the aesthetic appeal as does *Mālkaus* of *Hindustāni* music, even though identical notes and the same order of sequence are used. Similar is the case with *Chakravākam* in comparison to *Āhir-Bhairav* or *Subhāpantu-barāli* to *Todi*, or *Kalyāni* to *Yaman*, to mention just a few among many such cases.

Of the three customarily accepted varieties of performing art, Music has a special place since it is fully concerned with *Time* which leads the human soul to *Eternity*. Similarly paintings may be said to be concerned with space and thus to *Infinity*. But the arts which have reference to both space and time are *dance* and *drama*, and *dance-drama*. These are also called audio-visual art forms where *Eternity* and *Infinity* are said to melt into one *Whole*.

Dance is ordinarily understood to be the art which concentrates mainly on the delicate and the graceful movements of human body and the limbs in a very complicated but at the same time systematic rhythmic pattern bringing out a totality of either a devotional theme belonging to the life of *Krishna* or *Viṣnu* or other Deities and *avatāras*, or a pure and abstract rhythmic pattern of human postures (with no theme behind) with the help of systematic development of the movements of the limbs as required by the specific artistic impulse from within. Such abstract form of dance is usually accompanied by intricate and complicated drum beats by various percussion instruments in a variety of tempo constituting the basic background of the fundamental rhythmic totality which the specific dance event manifests.

The origin is traced to the *Tāndava* dance of *Siva* and the *Lāsya* dance of *Pārvati*. In *Chāndogya Upanishad* one can find references to Music, Dance and Drama. We need not enter into the details of the historical development or evolution of Dance or Drama as we have also avoided the issue of history elsewhere for the sake of relevance.

It will suffice to say that most of the forms and styles of dances in modern time are broadly divided into (a) *Kathak*, (b) *Bhāratnātyam*, (c) *Kathākali*. There are also other minor divisions. Besides the classical dance forms, we have a very large variety of folk dance prevalent in various parts of India most of which, if not all, are associated with some festivals—partly religious, but mostly cultural or social. They speak the spontaneity of joy of human heart, untrained but well-disciplined and highly systematic, the elements of discipline and system flowing freely from the emotional storage of basic human identification of man with his environmental commitments, never externally imposed. Folk dance of any variety is customarily attributed to the gay mood of the people. But it is never a case of intoxication or wild movements of hands and feet. There is always an element of sombre feeling manifested in these folk dances.

It is said that dance is the root of all arts. It is the manifestation of primal rhythmic cosmic energy of which *Śiva* is the main symbol with His diverse manifestations. Whatever be the origin, it is said to be the most obvious example of the activity of Gods which any form of Indian art or culture or religion cannot ignore.

According to Coomaraswamy[18] the dance of *Siva* represents His five-fold activities, namely creation or evolution, preservation or support, destruction (*the three major ones comprising the Supreme Trinity of the Indian Ideal*), veiling or illusion, and release or grace. The traditional portrait of the dance of *Natarāja* at once points to the empirical-transcendental dimension of Indian art. The image of one foot on the ground and the other foot off the ground respectively speaks of the immanent and the transcendent aspect of *Śiva*, the basic spiritual truth of human being.

Coomaraswamy[19] gives us the following quotation from *Chidaṃbara Mummani Kovai*:

> O my Lord, Thy hand holding the sacred drum has made and ordered the heavens and earth and other worlds and innumerable souls. Thy lifted hand protects both the conscious and unconscious order of Thy creation. All these worlds are transformed by Thy hand bearing fire. Thy sacred foot, planted on the ground, gives an abode to the tired soul struggling in the toils of causality. It is Thy lifted foot that grants eternal bliss to those that approach Thee. These Five Actions are indeed Thy Handiwork.

Coomaraswamy describes the grandeur of this conception as a synthesis of science, religion and art. To this we add that spirituality is the principle of such a synthesis. As supremely great, he continues, in *power* and *grace*, this dancing image must appear to all those who have striven in plastic forms to give expression to their intuition of Life, and all those are indebted to the saint-artists who first conceived such an image. This seems to be the basic point of convergence of all arts—verbal, performing and visual. Every part of this image is a symbolic expression of that *Energy* which science has to presuppose behind its theories, that *Grace* which religion has to express in all its rituals and ceremonies, that *Rhythm* which arts have to exhibit in their rendering of all works of creativity, whatever be the direction. "If we would reconcile Time with Eternity, we can scarcely do so otherwise than by the conception of alternations of phase extending over vast regions of space and grant tracts of time. Especially significant, then, is the phase of alternation implied by the drum, and the fire which 'changes' not destroys."[20]

The famous poem of Rabindranath on the dance of *Natarāja* is worth taking into account here. He, on the spiritual significance of this dance, composes the poem, which depicts the mysteries of His spontaneous creation in the existing ceaseless rhythmic flow of the sacred Ganges on whose shore music emerges from the very roots of her rhythm embracing the dawn of light in her bosom bringing the divine message of grace for the countless all who otherwise thought themselves to be eternally deprived of rest and peace—the meeting point of all for all ages.

Let us now add some brief remarks on Indian drama, one of the three components of the world of performing art.

It is said:

Na tajjnānam Na tatchhilpam Na Sā Vidyā Na sā kalā
Na sa yogo Na tatkarma Nātyeasmin Yanna dṛśyate

There is no knowledge, aesthesis, art, science, meditation or action the elements of which are not discernible in drama. We have normally two kinds of Indian drama—one is visual drama (*Dṛśya Kāvya*) and the other is verbal drama (*Śrāvya Kāvya*). The former actually belongs to performing art and the latter pertains to verbal art or literature or plays.

Normally it is accepted that the art of effective speech or elocution has its origin in *Ṛgveda*, that of music in *Sāmaveda* and that of acting in *Yajurveda*. The theory of *rasa* or of emotional essence is said to be rooted in *Atharvaveda*. What is known as *Nātya Śāstra* of *Bharata* is the primary source book on Indian art, though there is much debate regarding the writer himself, not to speak of the dates. *Manu* is said to be against the art of acting or dramaturgy because (being a strict moralist) he appears to be against such arts which he thought to be derogatory for the steady progress and moral stability of a society. But *Yājñavalkya* defended this art against the polemic of *Manu* and naturally we should acknowledge our indebtedness to him. Some critics have tried to discover a Western parallel in this context in the attitude of Plato and Aristotle respectively.

Nātya Śāstra is primarily concerned with the necessary directions and prerequisites for the actors enabling them to perform the function of acting true to the spirit of the relevant drama; it also contains some instructions for the dramatists who have the poetic vision to compose ideal dramas or plays.

Since drama as an art form involves a reference to both space and time together, the (aesthetic) senses involved are *seeing* and *hearing* together. The persons concerned are both audience and spectator. It may be mentioned here that unlike other art forms, namely, painting or music, drama as a performing art always requires a body of audience-spectator. A painter can draw his work of art, no matter if there is none to see or appreciate; a musician can compose or perform his own music in the solitude of his own even if there is none to listen. But the case of drama is different. It has its artistic significance (worth being designated as a form of art) in the presence of audience-spectator. Perhaps the same can be said, with some reservation, about dance. The case of divine dance would be, however, an exception.

Drama, in a broad sense, involves a four-fold performance: (a) *Āngika* or acting consisting in the movement of the parts of the body together with the appropriate expression of the face, particularly in the eyes of the actors and actresses (*Bharata* recognises the dramatic-aesthetic importance of the presence of women on the stage of performance); (b) *Vāchika* or acting consisting of the appropriate use of speech-organs; (c) *Sāttvika* or acting consisting of the appropriate emotional counterpart of the theme in the mind of the actors; (d) *Āhārya* consisting of materials like paints, dresses, ornaments and the like other than the psycho-physical organic constituents of the actors. Construction of the stage and the scenes of play also constitute an important part of the art of drama.

From the brief history of the multi-directional art forms of India ranging from the themes of the personifications of the forces of Nature, of Divinity, forces of basic and spontaneous human impulse in the interaction with Nature and with socio-cultural contexts to the visual (and non-visual also) interpretations of the pantheon of celestial beings, we can clearly see how the depth of spiritual experience of man has imprinted its profound and everlasting influence on Indian culture. Cross-cultural influence is also discernible in some cases; but the chief custodians of Indian art have always firmly stood against all counteracting forces in maintaining the main spiritual undertone in the country's age-old artistic heritage.

But *one word more*. The varieties of Indian art are never pursued as closed compartments. Music can be seen to influence painting and conversely; even Verse can be seen to influence music and be influenced by it—each is enriching and is being enriched by the other. In India, Rabindranath perhaps is the only outstanding torch bearer of the Indian artistic heritage where the three melt into one. In this context, a reference to Browning's poem can be made the title of which is the opening phrase of this paragraph. Unless one art form spontaneously bursts forth into another, no one art form in isolation is perfect in so far as spirituality is a multi-dimensional vital-conative impulse having an infinite range of appeal.

What of Rafael's sonnets, Dante's picture?
This: no artist lives and loves that longs not
Once, and only once, and for One only,
(Ah, the prize!) to find his love a language
Fit and fair and simple and sufficient—
Using nature that's an art to others,
Not, this one time, art that's turned his nature.
Ay, of all the artists living, loving,
None but would forego his proper dowry,—
Does he paint? he fain would write a poem,—
Does he write? he fain would paint a picture,
Put to proof art alien to the artist's,
Once, and only once, and for One only,
So to be the man and leave the artist,
Gain the man's joy, miss the artist's sorrow.

* * *

Oh, their Rafael of the dear Madonnas,
Oh, their Dante of the dread Inferno,
Wrote one song—and in my brain I sing it,
Drew one angel—borne, see, on my bosom!

The implication of Browning's poem is too obvious to explain or elucidate in the context of what has been already said. Whatever be the so-called domain of the artist, he has always one word more to say, his sorrow which perhaps can best be expressed through music when the artist's sorrow is fused with the joy of man.

Almost in a similar tone poet Rabindranath, the painter and the musician, sings in his poem *Gitānjali*:

> My song has put off her adornments, She had no pride of dress and decoration. Ornaments would mar our union; they would come between thee and me; their jingling would drown thy whispers.

> My poet's vanity dies in shame before thy sight, O master poet, I have sat down at thy feet. Only let me make my life simple and straight like a flute of reed for thee to fill with music.[22]

Yeats[23] correctly remarks in his introduction to *Gitānjali* (a collection of prose translations made by Rabindranath himself from his original Bengali poems):

These lyrics are full of "subtlety of rhythm, of untranslatable delicacy of colour, of metrical invention.... The work of a supreme culture... A Tradition where poetry and religion are the same thing." He further adds that Rabindranath, like Chaucer's forerunners, writes music for his words. And one realizes that he is so abundant, so spontaneous, so daring in his passion, so full of surprise that it had never been to anybody strange, unnatural or in need of any defence. *It is in Rabindranath that poetry, painting and music have reached one transcendent height, all together, where the cry of the flesh is inseparable from the cry of the soul.* "At the immortal touch of thy hands", says Rabindranath, "my little heart loses its limits in joy and gives birth to utterance ineffable."

This is how Indian religious culture with its depth of spiritual vision harmonizes and moulds music, painting and poetry in one absolute whole, the Absolute Reality which though present within us all, at once takes us away from the boundaries of the finitude and enables us to dive deep into that Transcendent mystery which is shining in its own glory and perpetually sending its message of inescapable invitation of Love and Joy where both the thorn of separation and the pleasure of union melt into the Elevated Supreme One.

Beyond time, place, and all mortality.
To hearts that cannot vary
Absence is Presence, Time doth tarry.
By absence this good means I gain
That I can catch her,
Where none can watch her,
In some close corner of my brain:
There I embrace and kiss her;
And so I both enjoy and miss her.[24]

We can realize that we have eyes to wonder, but lack tongues to praise,[25] when we behold these present days. We discover the soul and surrender to its spontaneity. We do not paint; we do not sing. Something from within makes us sing, makes us paint. Not that with a definite motive we seek for any hidden treasure, be it material or spiritual; we do not know how to cast our net. We only go forward—the endless adventure of existence without knowing the mystery of this pilgrimage, but only with the intrinsic voice in the infinity of human spirit.[26]

The universe of a painter or of a poet is more refined than that of our individual own. But the musician's universe may be said to be even more refined than that of the painter or of the poet. In defence of the acknowledged supremacy of the musician's universe, the following extract from Browning's[27] *Abt Vogler* appears worth quoting:

All through my keys that gave their sound to a wish of my soul,
All through my soul that praised as its wish flowed visibly forth,
All through music and me; For think, had I painted the whole,
Why, there it had stood, to see, nor the process so wonder-worth:
Had I written the same, made verse—still, effect proceeds from the cause.

Ye know why the forms are fair, ye hear how the tale is told;
It is all triumphant art, but art in obedience to laws,
Painter and poet are proud in the artist-list enrolled:

* * *

The poet proceeds further in visualizing music as the realization of the divine within man, the basic spiritual dimension of human being as such:

But here is the finger of God, a flash of the will that can,
Existent behind all laws, that made them, and, lo, they are:
And I know not if, save in this, such gift be allowed to man,
That out of three sounds he frame, not a fourth sound, but a star,
Consider it well: each tone of our scale in itself is nought;
It is everywhere in the world—loud, soft, and all is said:
Give it to me to use! I mix it with two in my thought;
And there! Ye have heard and seen: consider and bow the head:

* * *

Sorrow is hard to bear, and doubt is slow to clear
Each sufferer has his say, his scheme of the weal and woe;
But God has a few of us whom He whispers in the ear;
The rest may reason and welcome: 't is we musicians know.

* * *

This is how Browning sings his own song in praise of the musicians and of music as the whisper of God to few of us, the musicians alone. The obvious similarity of approach with the Indian classical music and particularly with the view upheld by Rabindranath would not perhaps require any further discussion.[28]

NOTES AND REFERENCES

1. Sri Aurobindo—*The Foundations of Indian Culture*, p. 236.
2. *Christian and Oriental Philosophy of Art*, p. 38.
3. It will be seen that there is a striking similarity of thought between Sri Aurobindo and Coomaraswamy.
4. *The Foundations of Indian Culture*, p. 237.
5. *Ibid.*, p. 240.
6. Rabindranath Tagore—*The Religion of Man*, p. 38.
7. *Ibid.*
8. *Personality*, pp. 28-29. By 'personality' Rabindranath never meant 'individual personality'; he rather meant 'personality of man' or in other words, the 'universal personality'. It is the '*personality*' where every individual *qua* individual can participate, but only at the cost of his own individuality being melted away. Coomaraswamy seems to be under a misconception about oriental art when he writes: our conception of art is essentially the expression of a personality, our whole view of genius, our impertinent curiosities about the artists' private life, all these things are the products of a perverted individualism and prevent our understanding of the nature of mediaeval and oriental art (p. 39, *Christian and Oriental Philosophy of Art*). It is no doubt true that Indian art and, in a sense, oriental art never encourages perverted individualism. But it is surprising how he, in the same breath, can choose to denounce the "artists' private life" along with the theory of art "as the expression of a personality". The two notions are basically different. The latter has and the former has no relevance in the context of Indian art. Moreover, the expression of a personality in art has very little, almost nothing, to do with the individualised style. He may be correct when he says that styles are the accident and by no means the essence of art. One can say that styles are accident and still hold the view that art is essentially the expression of a personality. To the question of style we shall come later on. Perhaps Coomaraswamy does not attach so much importance to the issue of personality in the context as does Rabindranath. But he is rather obscure, if not mistaken, on this point. He has confused 'style' with 'technique'. The latter is accidental; the former perhaps is not.
9. *Visva-Bharati Quarterly*, May 1942, p. 44.
10. W. Kandinsky—The Doctrine of Internal Necessity—a paper incorporated in *Creativity in the Arts* edited by V. Tomas.
11. *Ibid.*
12. *Personality:* Chapter on 'The World of Personality'.
13. D.W. Gotshalk—Paper on 'Form' as incorporated in *The Problem of Aesthetics* edited by Vivas and Kriegar.
14. For a detailed discussion of these principles and their associates the readers may consult the book as mentioned above.
15. *Op. cit.*, pp. 199-200.
16. The information is borrowed from Jogiraj Basu—*India of the Age of the Brahmanas*, p. 52.

17. The history of ancient Indian music is very complicated and our task here is not to reproduce a faithful history or a historical development of ancient Indian music. Our concern lies elsewhere. For the sake of relevance we have recorded some of the major items in the long and rich history of music in ancient India. Interested readers may consult for further information: Swami Prajnānānanda—*A History of Indian Music, Historical Development of Indian Music*; Arun Bhattacharya—*A Treatise on Ancient Hindu Music*; M.R. Gautam—*The Musical Heritage of India*. The source books written by *Bharata, Matanga* and *Śārangadeva* are considered to be most authentic and most informative to have a proper historical perspective. I acknowledge my indebtedness to all the sources mentioned here for the brief sketch which I have outlined here.

    Prof. Gautam in his *The Musical Heritage of India* (page 2) has recorded a somewhat different picture of the comparative table of *Vaidika* and *Laukika* (present day) notes as follows:

    Kruṣta (ma), Prathama (ga), Dvitiya (ri), Tṛtiya (sa), Caturtha (ni), Mandra (dha) and Atisvarya (pa).

    This appears to be more scientific, no doubt; but how far it is historically faithful is an open question for the professional musicologists to settle.

    Professor Arun Bhattacharya in his *A Treatise on Ancient Hindu Music* (page 23) has recorded a still different picture which is as follows:

    Prathama (madhyama), dvitiya (gandhara), tritiya (rishabha), caturtha (shadja), mandra (dhaivata), atisvarya (nishada), Krushta (pancama).

    The whole matter seems puzzling. Modestly I submit that I have been influenced by the serious research work on the mysteries of *Vaidik Svaras* by Prof. Ayodhyanath Sanyal (*Vaidik Svara Rahasya*) in recording the comparative table. This may appear to be acceptable to Swami Prajnānānanda. The occurrenee of *dha* and *ni* as mentioned in the book of Arun Bhattacharya seems to suggest that the scale followed in *Sāmagāna* is *vakra* or twisted and this was nothing unnatural at that period.
18. See his *The Dance of Shiva* for a detailed discussion.
19. *Ibid.*, p. 71.
20. *Ibid.*, p. 78.
21. R. Browning—One word more: borrowed from *A Selection of Poems*.
22. Rabindranath Tagore—*Gitanjali* (English Translation), p. 6; poem 7.
23. *Ibid.*: Introduction.
24. *The Golden Treasury*.
25. Shakespeare's 'To His Love' (borrowed from *The Golden Treasury*).
26. This is the view of Rabindranath Tagore.
27. R. Browning—'Abt Vogler'; borrowed from *A Selection of Poems*.
28. In her commentary on Browning's poem Mrs. Sutherland Orr remarks that Abt Vogler, the musician, consoles himself with the idea that music persists as an echo of the eternal life, a pledge of the reality, of every imagined good, of the continuance of whatever good has existed. It is sent up to Heaven to be continued and completed there. To this we may just add that Indian music is basically the same. It is the divine pilgrimage, the voice of God from within the man which elevates man and makes him cross the boundaries of this mundane world and enables him to open the gateways of the Divine abode.

CHAPTER 3

THE PHENOMENON OF MUSIC

In the context of Indian musicology,* it may not be perhaps undesirable to state in brief the origin of sound as expounded in the *Tāntrika* theory of creation in general.[1]

Broadly speaking the Trantras hold that creation begins with *Śabda* which is understood as the principle of Logos. *Śiva* or Brahman is said to have two aspects: *nirguna* or *niskala* and *saguna* or *sakala*. In the former aspect he is transcendent and beyond creation; in the latter he is associated with the principle of creativity which is otherwise called the principle of *Śakti*. Out of this *śakti* emanates *bindu* when there arises in *śakti* the desire to create. This is not a purposive desire. When *Śakti* comes in contact with *cit* or consciousness in her approach to light, *bindu* bursts and is divided. Out of this division we have *bindu, nāda* and *bija*. *Bindu* partakes of the nature of *Śiva* and *jñana; bija* partakes of the nature of *Śakti* itself and *nāda* is said to be the relation between the two as stimulator and stimulated (*kṣobha*). When *bindu* bursts there arises an incomprehensible volume of sound. This primordial sound is called *Śabda-Brahman* which is the fundamental cosmic sound potential. It is the source of all derivative sounds and the letters of the alphabet out of which words and sentences are made. From *śabda* there arises in the so-called ethereal regions *air* from touch, *fire* from colour, *water* from taste and *earth* from smell.

The derivative meaning of the term '*Tantra*' is said to refer to the theory which deals with the fundamental notion of *spreading* or *expanding* what is latent in the individual through consciousness in terms of knowledge

*It is a gross mistake to characterize Indian Musicology as *ethno*-musicology, as done by some foreign scholars.

as transcendental act.

'Tanyate vistāryate jñanam anena iti tantram'

In this context, what is relevant is to note that the cosmic sound potential is expanded into apparently disintegrated fractions of articulated sound on the basis of the frequency of the vibration in the air-particles. This presupposes *Varna* (in the *Tantras*) which does not mean letters of alphabet or colour, but means the *natural vibration* of the primordial object projected from perfect activity which is also otherwise called the '*Bindu*'. In this sense, *varna* can be said to determine and rule the order and harmony in creativity in the world of articulated sounds.

The traditional notion of *vistāra* (with the help of improvisation) which is an essential ingredient of Indian classical music may perhaps be traced to fundamental idea behind the philosophy of the Tantras in so far as the term *Tantra* has its root in *Tan* in the sense of *vistāra* which means *to spread*. Indian music is basically the *spread out* of the spiritual aesthetic vision of the musician and it is spontaneous emanation from within which intrinsically flows taking shapes in several specified music forms according to the demands of aesthetic creativity. Whether the form of improvisation technically called *Tān* can also be accepted to have been rooted in *Tan* is a serious issue for the scholars to decide. This much we can say that such an interpretation is very likely, even though it does not appear to have been sufficiently worked out.

To come back to our original question on sound. It is said that sounds are of two kinds—unheard and heard. The unheard sound is technically accepted in Musicology as *Anāhata Nāda* and heard sound as *Āhata Nāda*. The term *nāda* is accepted in its ordinary sense of sound as the vibration of air-particles. It is further said that only saints of high dedication can have access to *Anāhata Nāda*. The ordinary human beings have ability to deal with *Āhata Nāda* which is communicated to the human ear through an appropriate medium—the ear's natural anatomical construction.

The normal organ of hearing (ear) of adult human beings cannot catch sound vibration with a frequency of less than 20 per second or more than 20,000 per second.

Three factors are said to be necessary for our sensation of sound. The whole process of sound wave must start from a fundamental *vibrating source* which supplies energy to the surrounding medium through its intrinsic vibration. Secondly, the medium transmits the energy from the source to the receptor through sound waves. The receptor is the *receiver* which owing to its own constitutive capacity produces a sensation of sound. No sound can be transmitted through a vacuum. It can be transmitted through a material medium consisting of *mass* and elasticity, since sound waves involve compression and expansion.

The sensation of sound which we normally characterise as musical sound is produced by a regular succession of compression and the consequent rarefactions that the ear receives. The source will produce a musical sound (or *tone*) if the vibrations are regularly spaced. It must have a definite and fixed frequency. Sources which do not maintain a fixed frequency are not included within the class of musical sounds or *tones*, even though a sensation of sound may be produced. This may be technically described as *noise*, but not as a *tone*.

Pitch is the principal characteristic of sound by which it is assigned a particular place in a musical scale. In music, the determinant feature of pitch is the *frequency* of the sound wave or the rate at which the vibrating cause moves. For the same frequency, tones of very short duration have a lower pitch than those of longer duration. Increase in intensity raises the pitch of a high-frequency tone, but lowers the pitch of a low-frequency tone. The intensity of sound is a measure of its loudness. It is determined by the amount of sound energy (or the extent of the vibration called the *amplitude*) passing per unit area placed at right angles to the direction of propagation of the sound. The intensity of sound is a measure of loudness.

Timbre is another important characteristic by means of which we can distinguish two notes of the same intensity and pitch. If a sound having the same intensity and pitch is produced by two different instruments it is possible for us to differentiate the sounds according to their source instruments from which they are produced. The differentiation is possible owing to the corresponding different time-displacement *curves* from the different instruments concerned. The *curves* may have the same amplitude and *wave-length* having different *wave-forms*. In other words, two curves having the same amplitude may have the same pitch. But the *wave-form* may be different and this is what is meant by *timbre* or the quality of a musical sound. It depends on the specific *wave-form* which may otherwise be technically called *overtones*. This comes under the broad subject of *Harmonics* which, however, is beyond the scope of our present study.

It is important to observe here that when two musical notes are produced *together* and result in a pleasing sensation, the effect is technically called *concord* or *harmony*. Again, *concord* may be characterized as *melody* when two such notes are produced *one after the other* and the result is also an equally pleasing sensation. It is worth mentioning here that Western music, on the whole, is harmony dominated; but Indian music, on the other hand, is melody dominated. To this point we shall come back in the sequel.

The musical scale is commonly accepted as consisting of eight successive musical notes called an *octave* where the eighth note is regarded as the starting point of the next higher scale. These are, according to the Western musicians, *Do, Re, Mi, Fa, So, La, Ti—Do*: according to the Indian musicians, *Sā, Ri, Gā, Ma, Pa, Da, Ni—Sā*. According to Helmholtz, these are C, D, E, F, G, A, B—C.

This is customarily accepted as the Diatonic scale and is most widely used in performing music. The starting point is called the *tonic* or the key note.

The following is the standard diagram of the actual and the relative frequency of the notes on the scale:

(a) Helmholtz	C,	D,	E,	F,	G,	A,	B,	—C
(b) Western	*Do,*	*Re,*	*Mi,*	*Fa,*	*So,*	*La,*	*Ti,*	*—Do*
(c) Indian	*Sā*	*Ri,*	*Gā,*	*Ma,*	*Pa,*	*Da,*	*Ni,*	*—Sā*
(a) Actual Frequency	256,	288,	320,	341.3,	384,	426.7,	480,	512
(b) Relative Frequency	24,	27,	30,	32,	36,	40,	45,	48

We do not propose to enter into the details of musical acoustics. It will be, for our present purpose, enough to sum up the elements of a musical sound which are mainly three: (1) Pitch and rapidity of vibration, (2) Loudness and extent of vibration and (3) Timbre and the specific wave-form of vibration. In other words, musical tones are distinguished

(a) by their *length* of waves corresponding to *pitch* yielding the height or depth of sound;

(b) by their *amplitude* of waves corresponding to *loudness* or the *width* of sound; and

(c) by their *form* of waves corresponding to the *quality* of sound.

Thus the three major elements of a musical sound can be enumerated as follows:

1. Length
2. Width (Amplitude)
3. Form.

Sounds as heard cannot possibly have any other variety than of pitch, force or quality chronologically corresponding to the above table and analysed earlier,

No isolated note as such can produce music which is a *totality*, a *created* whole with a *creative* outlook. Notes of varying pitch and amplitude are introduced in music by individual musicians according to their own intrinsic vision to create emotive-aesthetic dimensions in their respective musical creations. A judicious combination of different notes and their interplay help to generate the desired effect blended with emotional embellishments.

Music is a living, dynamic phenomenon which acts as spiritual entrance to the higher world of human consciousness which comprehends mankind. It is beyond the total grasp of human intellect; it is that towards which man proceeds step by step by his own intrinsic necessity of feeling and willing. Music is not something which in its full form already *exists* in the external world. On the contrary, it is *not-yet-there* and has to be grasped by one's refined sense of intrinsic creativity. It is an ideal which does not only *push* the man from behind but *pulls* him in the front at a higher level. Man follows the *pull* until the *not-yet* is fully revealed to him. Thus music is without any beginning and without an end. Nobody knows when a man becomes a musician and nobody knows when a man ceases to be a musician. Music is the spontaneous artistic creativity of man; and art is without a beginning and without an end.

But what is the specific nature which distinguishes *music* from other art forms? The answer is found in the nature of the medium which the musician chooses. As has been already said, it is *sound*. Music is the *organization* of various sounds and their coordination according to some definite degree of proportion, balance and coherence. It is here that *music* differs from *noise* which is a chaotic and disorganized assemblage of sounds. A noise is hard and unmusical; it is *produced* by a shock or jerk of the air-particles. But a *tone* is smooth; its so-called nature is a repeated wave-movement of the air-particles which is *created* on the basis of rhythm.

It may happen that *tones* and *noises* appear together far more often than they appear separately and mix up very quickly. But their mixture is seldom complete enough to produce a simple sensation as that of *colour* or *brightness* does. The *tone* of a violin is said to owe a good deal of its effectiveness to the *noise* made by scraping the bow over the strings; but we are quite able to distinguish the scrape from the accompanying musical tone.[2]

A tone diagram may be said to resemble a spiral line (like a screw thread) with the deepest bass tone at the one end and on the other, the shrillest treble tone. The rest is arranged in a proportionate order between the two. Round each circle of the spiral are set the tones that we can distinguish within the limits of an octave. The vital point of a musical sound is that the line must be understood as spiral; it must keep returning as it advances towards the point which it started from, because the tones that bound an octave are more nearly like each other than any other two tones upon the scale. The noise diagram would resemble a straight line and there is no recurring likeness of noise to make the line a spiral.[3] Musical sound is characterised by a potential retardation along as it advances. The musical quality of sounds can be said to have a real basis. All sensations are pleasant only between certain limits of intensity. Human ears can easily discriminate between noise and tone, the former annoying and repulsive, and the latter having an undisputed charm. A sound is a musical tone if the pulsation of the air by which it is produced recur at regular rhythmic intervals. If there is no regular recurrence of waves, it is noise. The rapidity and smoothness of continuity of these regular beats determine the musical character of sounds. The ability to discriminate the various waves vibrating the air-particles is the condition of our finding music in sound, because every wave has its period. What we call a *noise* is a complication of sounds or notes too complex to decipher. Thus music is the principle of purity, regularity and balance in the sound waves which works on the basis of a harmonious and rhythmic compromise, and where this is absent music is lost and noise overpowers music.[4]

True proportion of the coordination of tones used in music cannot be calculated; organization of sounds with a proportion is what may be viewed as the *felt necessity* of the musician in accordance with his vision which is exclusively his own. There are indeed some broad boundaries, but they are never rigidly imposed upon the musician, because the musician, as a servant of art, is essentially free. His freedom is not one of *doing*, but one of *making*, a *creation* which is neither discovery, nor production, not even a construction. Music is a sort of projection of the musician's own image, his vision upon a canvas which does not exist as such, but exists in his own imaginative feeling according to his own impulsive inspiration (which is almost an imperative) with the help of an orderly and comprehensive sequence of notes. This will be developed in the sequel.

It is usually agreed that music consists of tones conveyed by instruments (or by human voice) in certain rhythmic and harmonic relations. But the question is there: whether music contains anything else, *i.e.*, ideas, emotions, will *etc.*; one may hold that music is primarily sounds in motion and does not mean anything; it does not refer to or represent anything outside music. But this seems to be an oversimplification. We have to see whether there is any meaning in music and what exactly it expresses.

It may appear that music deals not with the *reals*, but with the *unreals*, because music does not represent any *spatio-temporal configuration*. This is indeed true; but there is no harm either, because music is not without meaning, not without communication. Music as a genuine *art form* becomes meaningful by communication. The question naturally arises: What is it that music communicates?

Music does not communicate the *perceptions* or *natural experience* of the musician; it communicates his *spiritual attitude* which is deep rooted in the basic experience of his own life and realization. This higher consciousness of the musician is revealed by his innate capacity for ordering and organizing the notes (the chosen medium). It is the supreme power and innate capacity of the musician that the attitude he communicates to us is also felt by us to be valid and convincing; our response to music is the reaction to a more subtle and comprehensive contact with the reality than we can normally make. Thus a musician is said to be the *designer of a paradise* (Rabindranath).

Music is meant to *express* and not to *explain*. Explanation is not necessary, because the *communication* in music is self-explained in so far as it carries within itself an element of conviction—we are at once *one* with the musician in his higher domain of reality where he always struggles to find the meaning of his life. We share with the musician that transcendental state "where the struggle ends and pain dissolves away, although we know but little of his struggle and have not experienced this pain."[5] The musician lives in a universe richer than ours, a universe which is beyond the scientific scheme of things and events; but still it is his greatness that he makes us enter into his universe and realize his attitudes. Ultimately it is our own universe but as experienced and felt by a superior consciousness which is aware of its dignified dimensions, of which we cannot give a shape from our own feeling. The world of a musician differs from the world of an ordinary man, as the world of a man differs from that of an animal. The difference is one of *attitude*, though the materials constituting the world may be the same.

Thus music is always meaningful since it expresses and communicates an attitude, and in this way opens to us the doors of a higher and richer universe. Music is perpetually creative because it essentially contains within itself an element of surplus which overflows the limitations of time and space. It is always restless in its pursuit, its spiritual adventure of expression in the varied forms of self-realization. Music is the radiant revelation of man's personality which is unobscured by the shadow of self-interest. From the *details* to the *totality* is the growth and it is this *growth* which is *music*. It is this music which at once comprehends and transcends the details of this present empirical world. It is the renewal of the past and the signal for the future. Thus, we can distinguish a couple of aspects in music: (a) the aspect of law represented by the medium; (b) the aspect of will represented by the personality. The feeling and imagination of the musician *as dominated by his will* thrust him into the domain of rhythm; he chooses the sequence of sounds as the medium to express his realisation of rhythm and then becomes the "magician of rhythm who imparts an appearance of substance to the unsubstantial."[6]

A scientist *knows* the world as it exists; an ordinary man *perceives* the world as it appears, but the musician *feels* the world as it should be in accordance with his imagination; the world of the musician is a projection of his own attitude and it is this which he communicates with the help of an organized sequence of notes having a definite proportion, balance and harmony. The attitude of the musician is one of enjoyment and contemplation. He has not merely a *sympathy for* the world, but it is his *sympathy with*[7] the world through which he rises much above the average man and creates a richer world in which he lives.

Thus music communicates what cannot otherwise be communicated. This constitutes the uniqueness of music. Of course, every art form is unique. A painting, a sculpture or a poem—each is unique in its own way; there is no substitute for art. Art is no substitute for Nature, and arts are not substitutes for one another.

The strictly unique character of music consists in its presupposition of the reality of time. A painting exists in space, so is a sculpture. A poem on the other hand (a 'song' also may be included here) has reference to space because it is embodied in language which finds expression in space. But the case of music is different. The notes or the sequence of notes exist in time and they dwindle away leaving behind a *glorious past*; it is for the musician to revive and pick up the thread to create a total garland of sweet, fragrant flowers. Music is essentially this *totality* which is not at once given on the chosen canvas, but to be created; the *totality* is the totality of *vision* which is at once before the musician's imagination and to this *total vision* the musician gives a proportionate shape stage by stage, progressively, following the same thread which runs through the creation in its fullness of life. Music is unique because the thread is never broken; it is like a flowing stream with *newness* and *spark* at every stage, with no repetition or imitation of the past. Every *past* is renewed into the *present* and every present is transformed, carried over to the *future* with an excellent skill of imagination towards a total achievement. Music is like a tree "which has its inner harmony and inner movement of life in its beauty, its strength, its sublime dignity of endurance, its pilgrimage to the unknown through the tiniest gates of reincarnation. The creative genius cannot stop exhausted; more windows have to be opened."[8] The brute facts of material world might create obstacles to the musician's universe. But these initial prohibitions are transcended by the musician and the frontiers are *triumphantly crossed.*

The reality of time as presupposed by and involved in the phenomenon of music is not the uni-directional time as recognised by the philosophers and the physicists. On the contrary, it has two directions. The *no-longer* note, though literally no longer, is not totally extinguished. Similarly, the *not-yet* is not entirely new. The luminous present has one direction to the future as *expectation to be fulfilled* and another direction to the past to be revived as being capable of *fulfilling the expectation.* Music is a continuum which is non-unilinear and here time operates in a unique, spiral dimension. The appropriate phrase seems to be *circular dimension* in which time operates and constitutes the continuum by virtue of a combination of centripetal and centrifugal direction. The linear notion of time may be misleading in case of music since it carries with it an idea of irreversible series of events moving along a line from past to future. Music is the projection of orderliness into what is not irreversible, for then, the *totality* would vanish.

The musical notes permit not only of reconstruction but also of reordering and reversal, permutation and retrograde of past notes.

The notion of linear time and that of causality are usually held to be inseparable. But along with the notion of linear time, the notion of causality is also cancelled in music. In musical time, one event or a note cannot be said to cause the next one; every note is original and spontaneous. The phenomenon of music is basically a resurrection, an exhumation of the past giving birth to a luminous abiding present, the whole in its full life.

On the basis of the transitory fleeting notes of sound, the musician creates the superstructure of an all-pervasive tonal unity which answers to his own totality of vision. The details of the notes used have no meaning in isolation—they are meaningful only in respect of the totality which the musician creates. Thus the musician in his imagination realises his individual spirit to be in a union with a spirit which is everywhere. Morning does not wait for a scientist to reveal itself. Similarly the imagination of a musician does not wait for any external adjustment of isolated, temporal, evanescent facts in the external world. He realizes that peace and tranquillity are the essences of harmony which dwell in nature. He also realises that this harmony *carries an eternal assurance of his spiritual relationship to reality which waits for its perfection in his musical creativity.*

Music reveals man's spiritual wealth of life. It seeks its freedom in forms of perfection which are ends in themselves. Music is perpetually creative since it contains within itself the spiritual power of organizing improvisation bursts forth from his self-realization or the sense of identity between himself and the musical theme which he is lost into. This is what is meant when it is said that a musician is born and is lost in his creation. Creation is not just performance; it is the intuitive recollection of what is already *felt within*—the pure, essential form of music,—the internal structure, the vital and the spiritual core of man.

Music has thus a characteristic *openness* subject to infinite interpretations. In this sense, there is no difference between Indian and Western music. Music is of the *human Soul* where the Indians and the Europeans are all alike. Musical form always remains as the pure form to be realized by oneself within oneself alone. What is *real* has to be *realized* and what is realized may be *represented* through the current laws of society, culture and history. But musical form is never confined to such laws. It is rather determined by the law of inner human necessity which constitutes the essence of musical creativity. Instead of being determined by the so-called laws of society and culture, it is music which itself determines the laws of society and culture, and thus creates a history. Music is not subservient to history; but rather history is subservient to music.

Music as a work of art is a continuous renewal. If a musician prefers self-repetition, then there is an end in his music. The attitude of a musician is one of obedience to an inner necessity which takes him beyond the boundaries of his own limitations as an individual human being within a definite perspective, and leads him on to a higher perspective where he realizes the fulfilment of his own impulsive necessity, a constant drive towards self-expansion, a *higher Soul*. This inner necessity is the music in its *pure intrinsic* form which is not *representative* of anything, but *unique* and is, in this sense, purely formal and purely universal. The purity and the intrinsicness of such musical form cannot be calculated, nor can be clearly translated into ordinary language. It has genuine proportion, harmony, consistency and comprehensiveness. Proportions *etc.* are within the musician's vision and are not externally imposed upon him.

The laws of proportion and consistency are the laws of human sympathy, laws of human Soul with which a musician is born, and as such the laws are innate. Such laws cannot be properly theorised. In music theory does not, however, precede, but may follow.* A realization has a spontaneous expression through any medium as the artist chooses and in this respect he is absolutely free. The general structure of such laws can be formulated later on, but there is always an additional *vital core*

*This point has been developed in the Chapter on Rāga and Rasa.

to simply an emotion of *melancholy* or of *joy etc*. Such emotions, if at all admissible in music, enter into the total effect but never figure as isolated elements. The total effect may be described as *ecstasy* which is much higher than the so-called human emotions of simple *joy* or simple *pleasure* or *grace etc*. Music reveals the *luminous joy* because it is the self-unfoldment of the musician which is self-evident inasmuch as it is self-creative. It is the felt immediacy which has a spiritual spark. The essence of music thus consists in carrying the entire mankind into a feeling of *oneness*, an identity which unifies the musician, the listeners and the music which is created.

The components of a musical phenomenon may be roughly enumerated as consisting of (a) intuition, (b) inspiration, (c) concentration and (d) faith. The intuitive attitude of a musician towards his own experiences of life and Nature grows out of an inspiration from within which is further enriched by his concentration and faith in his own intrinsic capacity to formulate and unify by well-ordered sequence of tones, wherein the tones blend in order to strengthen and enrich each other, and a *meaning* emerges. The musician is the *impartial spectator* with an original vision who introduces reality into what is otherwise unreal. This world is not the pre-existent world of ordinary man. This is a world of miracle every temporal fraction of which is witnessed by us on the basis of interrelations of notes which the musician projects upon a self-created canvas, and a magnificent world is gradually revealed before us of which we had no experience before. Music is a disclosure of a miraculous world which absolutely rests on itself having its own foundation characterized by a *spiritual growth* of which the human counterpart is his *eternal surplus* always beyond, always *to be* achieved, the *eternally transcendent* based on unspeakable imagination. When music makes us enter into the Infinite silence, we at once realize that silence is more eloquent than speech, and this is the magical power of musical sound.

The image with which the musician proceeds in his artistic creauvity is more than the sum of its elements. It is its characteristic spontaneity out of which a new phenomenon flashes forth and this is music which is comparable to nothing else. To listen to a piece of music is, similarly, to listen it imaginatively without the help of any analogue. The reality of music consists in the depth and richness of the imagination from either side. The listener is also a potential musician, because he has to proceed strictly as music proceeds; he grows with the growth of music; he dances with the rhythm of music.

The canvas of a painter is a two-dimensional real entity upon which he uses line and colours and introduces a new dimension which together exists in space. But the canvas upon which the musician works is his own creation and this is creation in time—a single dimensional entity—namely, duration. Upon this self-created canvas, the musician weaves the network of purely temporary sounds and by a superb skill of manipulation projects his attitude upon the temporary canvas with the help of temporary sounds. The created canvas and the creative projections together build up a miraculous world where the distinction is necessarily blurred and a totality floats which is the real world of music based on otherwise unreal elements.

Music reveals to us not this or that aspect of reality, this or that mode of being, this or that joy or sorrow. It reveals the essential nature of all joys and sorrows, the nature of all being. Yet it is not absolutely abstract since it creates a tremendous human reaction whereby man is swayed away in forgetting his own individual identity, in being lost in the richer identity which prevails and unifies the musician with his own music. The same, to some extent, applies to the listener also.

In music we find a representation of the man's world as a whole. It stands alone, quite cut off from all the other arts. In it we do not find the copy or repetition of any Idea of existence in the world. We must attribute to music a far more serious and deep significance connected with the innermost nature of the world and our own self. The other arts may be said to objectify the *Will* indirectly only by means of the *Ideas* and thus are inseparably linked with the phenomenal world. But music can exist if there were no world at all. It is as direct an objectification of the whole *Will* as the world itself.[11] This objectification may rather be characterized as the humanization of the whole universe. Music is thus the *empathy* of the human will. It is the keynote for humanizing the objects to which music by itself does not belong. Artistic enjoyment is the enjoyment of a sensible object. But music is an enjoyment where the enjoying ego is objectified, a kind of objectified self-enjoyment. The *self-enjoyment* is the *human will* in action arising out of a life beyond. The act of will is not the cause of the action, but is the action itself. "We need a foothold for the will in the world. The will is an attitude of the subject to the world. The subject is the willing subject.... If the will has to have an object in the world, the object can be the intended action itself. And the will does have to have an object..... The wish precedes the event, the will accompanies it...... Idealism singles man out from the world as unique, solipsism singles me alone out, and at last I see that I too belong with the rest of the world, and so on the side *nothing* is left over, and on the other side, as unique, *the world*...... As my idea is the world, in the same way my will is the world-will."[12]

Music is thus the Supreme Will in action which comprehends and *humanizes* the whole world and reveals a richer world where man lives his life in music. The will seems always to have been related to man's feeling and imagination, because we cannot *imagine* that we have carried out an act of will without at the same time having *felt* that we have carried it out. The ultimate object of will is always the aesthetic object, the *beauty* and the *sublime* in the humanized world.[13]

NOTES AND REFERENCES

1. The following account of the Tantras is borrowed from Manoranjan Basu—*Fundamentals of the Philosophy of Tantras: Tantras—a General Study*. The detailed study of the Tantras: as the basis of Indian music is immensely vast and requires a completely separate treatment. Inquisitive readers may go through the original texts on this subject and other treatises which are available. We have mentioned only a brief and elementary account of the origin of sound just to get an entry to our discussion.
2. Titchener, E.B.—*A Primer of Psychology*, p. 43.
3. *Ibid.*
4. Santayana, G.—*The Sense of Beauty*, p. 45.
5. Sullivan, J.W.N.—*Beethoven*, p. 23.
6. Rabindranath Tagore—*Art and Aesthetics*, p. 49.
7. The terms are borrowed from K.C. Bhattacharya—*Studies in Philosophy*.
8. Rabindranath Tagore—*The Religion of Man*, p. 17.
9. Rabindranath Tagore—*Art & Aesthetics*, p. 55.
10. Sullivan, J.W.N.—*Beethoven*, p. 36.
11. This interpretation is borrowed from Schopenhauer, A.—*The World as Will & Idea*, pp. 330-31 (Vol. I).
12. Wittgenstein, L.—*Note Books* (1914-1916), pp. 85-88.
13. This chapter and the following one are the revised versions of an earlier draft of my paper published in *Visva-Bharati Quarterly, Ramkinkar Issue*—1983. In revising the draft of my paper I have tried to incorporate the suggestions of Prof. A.R. Kelkar, Poona and Dr. E.S. Perera of the Department of Instrumental Music, Rabindra Bharati University, Calcutta.

CHAPTER 4

MUSIC AND MAN

Man lives and works within a framework of fundamental values, *Truth, Beauty* and *Goodness*. The first is known as intellectual value, the second as aesthetic value and the third as moral value. There is a constant interaction between these values by virtue of which each of these is enriched and attains a full dimension in the total make up of man in his relation to Nature. An *individual* thus grows into a *person*; and a *person* grows into a *man*. What we mean by culture or civilisation of a nation is basically the input and output mechanism between man and nature with reference to these values, the contribution of which is reflected in and thus constitutes the life and growth of a culture. As pointed out earlier Indian culture is rooted in the spiritual vision of man which works in the background for the perpetual interplay of these values in the total perspective of man and nature.

To be beautiful or *to appreciate beauty* is man's birthright. Thus one may be inclined to say that of the three fundamental values, beauty reigns supreme. An object of beauty to which all men are indifferent would be regarded as a contradiction in terms. Beauty is a positive value in so far as it is associated with a positive state of enjoyment, the state of feeling and willing together. That man is endowed with a sense of beauty is his pure intrinsic treasure. "If colour, form, and motion are hardly beautiful without the sweetness of the odour, how much more necessary would they be for the sweetness itself to become a beauty."[1] Beauty is the co-operation of pleasures and consists of the objectification of pleasure. In other words, it is pleasure or enjoyment self-objectified.

Man can afford not to be truthful, or he can afford not to be moral; but Man cannot afford not to be beautiful. A man who does not know what is truth or what is morality, still knows what is beauty in his day-to-day life. A man untrained in any intellectual discipline knows or appreciates the beauty of a flower, of the rainbow in the sky or of the sunset. A man knows how to make himself beautiful according to his own internal sense of proportion. In other words, *beauty* consists in proportion, and degrees of beauty consist in the degrees of proportion, in relation to the elements of the thing which it consists of or involves any reference to.

The value framework within which a man lives may thus be interpreted to lead to the *triumph of beauty*. But it must at the same time be mentioned that *beauty* cannot be understood in total isolation from *truth* and *goodness*. That all the three values are very closely interlinked can be established by citing a reference to Epics, to the works of great artists which have become the objects of legendary fame or the poems of great visionaries who remain immortal through their literary creations.

What is beautiful remains at the very beginning a matter of the senses. But the inner realization drives the man onwards to pass beyond the limits of the senses. The transition is always a matter of degree and not of kind; and man, through his appreciation of the beautiful, tends always to overcome the limits of his finitude to enter into the kingdom of the Infinite. Since a man is conscious of his limits, he is equally conscious that as a man he has to transcend the limits. It is said by the Idealist Philosophers (John Caird, for example) that the knowledge of a limit involves the potential transcendence of it. Man must know what exists outside, beyond his limits, and is thus limiting himself from outside.

In his conscious attempt to rise above his own limitations, man is constantly rushing forth to overcome his own limitations, only to get merged into the joy of the union with the Infinite, the Supreme Being; call it *Divinity* or *Pure Consciousness* or *Pure Bliss*, does not matter. Whether the total progress of the development or enrichment of human existence as such is always a conscious process at every stage is very difficult to say. But one thing is clear that so long as a man is conscious in his aesthetic enjoyment being within the boundaries of his senses, he has *aesthetic appreciation*; but when he feels the compelling necessity of forgetting about the senses he has entered into *aesthetic involvement*, and when he is lost within himself he has reached the stage of *aesthetic realization*. It is at this stage that the aesthetic attitude reveals itself into the spontaneous creativity of the artist through new and new forms depicting new and new enrichment of higher-order realizations. Why an artist prefers to *create*, nobody knows; perhaps the artist himself does not know; perhaps the very question is illegitimate. *Why the flower blooms*, or *why the wind blows*, or *why the river flows* is something which *nobody knows*. It is something spontaneous, a case of revitalization of the very nature of existence through new and new forms which do not have to obey any fixed rules. The creations themselves are the rules which are on a par with the laws of nature or the laws of the cosmos.

Music is primarily a performing art. It represents the *inexhaustible magnificence* of our creative spirit which spontaneously manifests itself in the style of composition or improvisation which is unique in its manner and universal in its appeal. It carries within itself its own criterion of excellence being the outcome of the spiritual realization of the Infinite within Humanity. Herein lies the secret of Indian music which is beyond all calculation or grammatical formulation. It has its own grammar in the sense that it is never whimsical; its grammar is oriented by the inherent discipline and harmony between human feeling and willing. The musician always feels a necessity of obedience and faithfulness to the intrinsic structure of any particular musical theme, the emotional core of musical creativity. But this feeling of obedience is never mechanically imposed; it comes out of the realization of the musician himself who is absolutely free to choose any medium for the expression of his own realization. This freedom is not one of *doing*, but of *making* which is characterized by a unique creativity which combines both skill and talent through a long period of ascetic preparation which helps the musicians not only to develop the medium of expression and the style of presentation, but also to eliminate the influence of the so-called obstacles of *imitational urges*.

Music is a progressively living phenomenon which is characterized by its incessant flow expressing itself in infinite number of compositions or improvisations on a rigorous and disciplined basis strictly in accordance with the intrinsic law of human feeling and imagination. If the upholders of any musical tradition do not make ample provision for the growth and development of music, then they are not to be regarded as genuine musicians. The value of any musical tradition thus consists in: (a) adaptation to the present socio-cultural environment and, (b) survival of the fittest, subject to a verdict, spiritually inclined towards artistic creativity. Any musical tradition should never be allowed to be a closed-door institution; rather it should have both *entry* and *exist*—the former unbiased, unsophisticated and the latter purified, enriched and ever-radiating. To this point we shall come again in our discussion on the Musical Traditions of India.

At this stage, we have the total man who has transcended the surface character of all values, their superficiality, and has taken them all in a higher level, the level of the sublime. From the three so-called values taken in one unified whole emerges the *creative man* through his self-transcendence. Reality is truth; truth is eternal; the eternal is the Highest Good, the Highest Good is the Supreme Value which is the *Sublime*. It is only through the realization of the *beautiful as the sublime* that man can establish his communion with the Divine Supreme Being towards which he is constantly rushing forth. The beautiful is pleasant, but the sublime is self-enhancement because of the greatness and the overwhelming astonishment which a man cannot but to surrender to. The tendency of man is a *quest for* and a *conquest of the Great, the Supreme* only by surrender; *we lose to win, we die to live, we end to start.*

Music is *not the beautiful in art*, but *the sublime in art*. It is the voice of the human soul which is spontaneously expressed through the language of the heart with the medium of sound as eternally self-creating. In music, the emphasis is on *sublimity* and not on *beauty*. In case with the former, one can discern an element of the feeling of purposiveness of the object in its relation to the subject; in case with the latter there is a feeling of purposiveness of the subject in relation to the object which involves a harmony of the mental powers. In case of the beautiful, the mind is at rest; but in case of the sublime, there is an excitement, a mental movement, a growth of the mind along with the growth and development of the phenomenon concerned. Music is a living phenomenon with a characteristic growth towards a finality which is never achieved because of its inherent ceaseless dynamism. Music is lost, if the dynamism is lost.

In view of its spontaneous flow of creativity, music makes us aware that as natural beings we are not only independent of Nature, but superior to Nature. Music has an infinity of extension; it is high and exalted; it opens before us a vast horizon including the great and powerful forces of Nature on the basis of the supremely rich potential of sound creating in man the feeling of *identification* and of *transcendence* which can be described as the *real freedom* of man. It is here that mind is confronted with the sublime. The aesthetic object in music is not an entity, but a situation with a focus which has to be transcended. In this transcendence, the focus is lost and creates an enriched situation which, again, involves an element of transcendence.

Music as an art form is an end in itself, and not a means to an end, A musician *is born* and not *made*. It is the voice of intuition and not of intellect. Intellect may follow and enrich the intuitive verdict; but it cannot replace what is intuitively realized.

The dominant characters of the *form* in Indian classical music, which it is very difficult to describe in ordinary language, might be regarded as the *improvisation* which means that every musician is both a creator, a composer and performer; the creativity which is the keynote of the temporal units into a super-temporal, eternal sublimity. Music is a totality which starts with a suspense and ends in a feeling of awe and reverence which sweepingly takes man beyond the boundaries of space and time.

The first stage of suspense may be described as a negative state of being checked or repelled; but such a stage immediately rushes forth to the next stage of uplifting and self-expansion which ends in a positive state of the feeling of union with the total musical phenomenon, enabling man to transcend his own limitations into an organic relation with eternal, spiritual values characteristic of the Divine creation.

Music is said to be the finest and purest of all art forms because it dwells permanently within some purely abstract temporary sounds, skilfully organised. If you try to understand what life is by analysing a living being, you will find tissues, nerves, blood cells, nitrogen and so on; but you will miss *life* for ever. Similarly, you cannot find music by analysing the temporary notes. The life of music lives in the totality beyond the purely temporal and herein lies the uniqueness of the vision of the musician. Music makes permanent what is otherwise purely temporary; it makes real what is otherwise unreal. It can be compared with a dew drop which "is a perfect integrity that has no filial memory of its parentage."[9] Music is created by a subtle principle of rhythmic distribution of temporal notes among themselves; its character is in its massive movement, its incalculable potentials. It *grows*, but it is never *there* before us. It is the depth and the subtlety of the musician's vision which works as the principle of growth.

Music differs from other forms of art in another important aspect. A poet or a painter cannot express his reaction or attitude to any situation without mentioning the situation; but a musician can do. In music, the situation is irrelevant; one can read a situation into a piece of music, but that would be superfluous; one has to rise above situational perspectives. One must have a direct access to the musician's universe which is self-sufficient and needs no further explanation. "Music, compared with the other arts, is a kind of disembodied ghost, and has all the advantages and disadvantages of that state."[10] Thus the so-called content of music is not the situation, but the musician's attitude or reaction to any situation of his own life, the projection of his own life upon an empty, non-real canvas, a canvas which does not exist at all, in the ordinary sense of the term.

Psychologists have tried to classify human emotions by putting different labels. But it is difficult to fully characterize an emotion as evoked by a piece of music. No music can be adequately described as giving rise which constitutes the life of music, the creation of the artist. Thus music as pure form is both objective and subjective, both universal and individual; it is subjective and individual because it has an expression which has an impact upon the ages creating a history or a tradition of its own.

As man is potentially divine in his inborn attempt to rise above his limitations which are only superficially human; so it is the right of every art form to be intrinsically divine, because art is always an attempt at humanization of the Divine. The task of the musician (or of every artist whatever be the medium of expression) is to establish a *total community feeling* with the listeners or the connoisseurs. Art is never meant for being only appreciated or enjoyed by others. Exhibitionism in art is thus forever prohibited; it only destroys, but never augments the artistic spirit.[2] The real has to be realized within oneself. This is a *must* not for the artist alone, but also for the public who are interested in the works of art. In other words, *to realize the real* is art, and it is here that feeling of being in *one community* can be attained. The success of a musician lies in producing such a feeling—where the artist is lost in his creative artistic expression and the listeners are lost in the creation by the artist. What shines above everything in its own glory is not *the beautiful,* but *the sublime* in music. This, in other words, may be regarded as the realization of the *Divine* within *Man.* The actual performance of the musician should not be and actually is not influenced or conditioned by any idea of aesthetic approval; rather, the main concern always is and should be to take the listeners out of their bounds and carry them along with his own self-realization towards the path of communion with the Divine which is always within the man himself.

It is in music that man fully expresses himself. Music is the canvas upon which man projects his own realizations which are spontaneous outcomes of his own feeling and imagination. The inherent dynamism of music identifies the canvas with the projections so that the *projections* and that upon which the *projections* are made become indistinguishable. This constitutes the *purity* of music as an art form. Music is a phenomenon where man, the canvas and his projection become all in one. The so-called *rāgas* of Indian music may be chosen here as examples of the so-called canvas upon which the musical structure is created by projecting notes of sound in ordered sequence. But the canvas is not already there for the musician to start with as it is in the case of a painter. The musical canvas is a potentiality which is gradually revealed in its full form along as the musician gradually proceeds with his projections, his own realization of the notes and their sequence. The canvas and the product are created simultaneously and spontaneously and in this total creation the musician loses himself by transcending his limited existence. "Man is all the time outside of himself: it is in projecting and losing himself beyond himself that he makes man to exist; and, on the other hand, it is by pursuing transcendent aims that he himself is able to exist. Since man is thus self-surpassing, and can grasp objects only in relation to his self-surpassing, he is himself the heart and centre of his transcendence."[3]

Man in his musical creativity creates a new universe which is much richer and more elevated than the natural universe, because the musician and the listener together form an integral part of a community which is the real human universe. The secret of this communion lies in the magical powers of music which has a triple dimension: (a) it has an identity of the canvas and the projections upon the canvas; (b) it has an identity of this totality of projections and the projector, the musician himself and (c) it has an identity of the musician and the listener.[4] These three dimensions are not really distinct; they together constitute the life and soul of music, its inherent growth and its spontaneous flow towards higher and higher achievements merging into spiritualism which is the characteristic transcendence and freedom of man as man. It is not by "turning back upon himself, but always by seeking, beyond himself an aim which is one of liberation or of some particular realization that man can realize himself as truly human."[5] Music is the *aim* which man looks beyond himself and it is through music that man *realizes* himself, *transcends* himself and *becomes free.* The *man* in the musician is his music; the *music* in man is his own realization as man, his transcendence, his freedom; the freedom in man is his spiritualism, an attitude which takes man upwards to a richer universe. This is not subjectivism; it may rather be described as *subjectivity* which is universal and has its own *certitude.*

It is the element of *felt-certitude* which makes the *subjectivity* impersonal; in other words, it carries the musician beyond his personal values and the musician by virtue of his freedom becomes *freely impersonal.* Thus, music is both subjective and objective because the phenomenon of music has a two-directional aspect: (a) it is *subjective* in so far as it has an assimilative and abstractive direction (abstraction from the concrete sensuous experiences of the natural world), and (b) it is *objective* in so far as it has a *projective* or *creative* direction (projection of the attitude of the musician in revealing a richer universe).* In music, the self-consciousness is the *Heart Universal* where the feeling of the

*This point which has been mentioned earlier has also been further taken up in the Chapter on Rāga and Rasa.

musician is eternalized as the realization of an eternal value; it is this value which works as the *core-principle* of identification of the musician with his music.

Music involves a constant dissociation from the empirical values and at the same time a commitment to real eternal values. These two elements of dissociation and commitment together constitute the *felt-person-in-general* which is at the background of the *Heart Universal* which is the essence of music.[6]

The subjective-objective process in music may thus be explained following the lines as suggested by Prof. K.C. Bhattacharya:

> When one is only trying to enjoy, the feeling has indeed begun; but there is a constant sense of not being able to enjoy, of the object refusing to be enjoyed, to melt into the feeling. This tantalizing experience constitutes the unreal character that attaches to the incipient feeling. To successfully enjoy, to have the object dissolved in one's feeling, is to get rid of the felt unreality. The feeling here becomes subjectively real; it stands by consuming the object.[7]

This is the struggle which a musician has to fight out in his creativity and music flows when the struggle is over in favour of the musician. In this way, the musician identifies himself with his music which stands as the eternal value itself. This is the prize which the musician fights out of his struggle with Nature, and projects in a new world where the eternal value shines in its own glory as transcendent from the momentary empirical values.

The so-called '*performer-listener*' dichotomy is a misleading, rather faulty, approach to understand the phenomenon of music in its fullness. If any listener fails to appreciate a piece of music, the fault is his own and not that of the performer. He is not a listener of music, because he has failed somewhere to pursue the running thread by which the performer took up the *no-longer* past note and rolled on to the *not-yet* future notes through the *gracious present*. What he has listened to are some arbitrary sounds which account for his failure to appreciate music which is an *organic continuum*. He is a real, genuine listener who can keep equal pace with the musician in his development of the sequence of notes, and once he is successful in this much needed task of a listener, the dichotomy disappears.

The subjective-objective attitude which is discernible in a musician in his performance is what is discernible also in a painter or in a poet. It is not here that the essence of music can be found out. This, however, can be said to consist in the *temporal-eternal* elements which the musician by his genius can combine into a *projected totality*. The temporal is raised and realized as *sub specie aeternitatis*. This is what constitutes the uniqueness and supremacy of music as distinguished from all other forms of art. The *temporal present* manifests itself within the created totality as the *eternally present*, as the *universal moment*.

Music thus can be said to occupy all the room between man and nature; it does not have a definite starting point. It is like the empty, clear blue sky in its total vastness. In the boundless blue sky of musical domain the conventional attitudes of localisation and juxtaposition melt away in a higher fusion of *tones* in their orderliness and coherent manifestation. Music is rather the abstract world of man consisting of ordered sounds in which *time* is but the principal medium in and through which the notes are sensed to move in whatever direction as deemed fit for the enrichment and purification of the musician's universe.

Music is the discovery of the *noumenon* in the *phenomena*, of the *real* in the *appearances*, of the *transcendent* in the *empirical*, of the *objective* in the *subjective*, of the *depth* in the *surface*, of the *vertical* in the *horizontal*, and particularly of the *eternal* in the *temporal* (wherein lies the uniqueness of music, the preceding ones being discernible in other forms of art). Music is the projection of human attitudes as felt from within upon a canvas which is not pre-existent but is created along with the projections themselves. The canvas figures in music as the very principle of projectibility and music is *projectibility projected, creativity created*. Music is a sort of phenomenon which does exist; but it exists *nowhere*, because it always exists *now here;* it is the shining present which dominates the *not-yet* and the *no-longer* by a balanced, proportionate and continuous sequence into which the notes are sewed through. It is always a development, a growth which is spontaneous and progressive ending itself into a comprehensive totality of a richer life. Along with his music the musician passes through a progressive development of his mind which closes for the time being in an achieved end where his *felt attitudes* are, to some extent, realized in an emergent eternal value which is, however, always in need of further enrichment and revitalisation.

Music unfolds to us a world of *forms* and *essences* whose final picture is the outcome of a sort of spiritual growth. The *will* in a moral context is relevant for the freedom of man in his *doing*, but the *will* in a musical context reveals the man in his freedom of *making*, which acquires a long ascetic preparation by virtue of which the musician is able to overcome the obstacles of his impulses, perceptual experiences, acquired habits and others allied to these. The internal necessity to which a musician has to submit is a sort of spiritual necessity, its laws being the laws of human sympathy. The necessity is the necessity of his *free will* in and through which the musician creates the magnificent superstructure of his music (which imparts a nearly definite shape and form to his own attitudes) based on the sequences of notes upon the stuff. Music is thus faithful obedience to the *spiritualism in man* which is his *freedom,* the medium of expression of such obedience being the tones. The result of the inner necessity of feeling and willing finds expression in an evergrowing sense of balance, harmony and proportion which the musician makes use of in his creativity. The so-called finality in any piece of music is arbitrary. Music does not suffer from any limitation. The musician is always free to choose any form which his inner inspiration finds suitable; and finality is a word foreign to music.

The musician's universe may be said to be characterized by the principle of: (a) ontological detachment, (b) teleological enterprise and (c) spiritual commitment. The universe, however, has a cosmological perspective transcendentally inclined. A musician, in his obedience to the laws of intrinsic necessity which, as we have seen, are the laws of human sympathy, has to dissociate himself from the ontological situation which is responsible for his isolated perceptions and experiences. The dissociation is necessary because the attitude of the musician with which he begins is in need of conquering the potential dangers which act as obstacles arising out of blind impulses and crude perceptions rooted in the ontological situation. The enterprise has to be teleological, because the musician has, though not always consciously, an end in view, namely, to give expression to his own realization on the basis of his chosen medium. It is not pragmatism, since a true musician never brings down or should never bring down his music to the gross satisfaction of the general listeners. The commitment is spiritual, because the realization of the musician is meaningful only in a spiritual context which consists in the exaltation and augmentation of his feelings and imagination to a higher and richer world than that in which he lives his empirical life pragmatically oriented. These three principles taken together will roughly account for the perspective where the entire cosmos is revealed before his vision which is a universe of more and more refined and purified values, the truly eternal beyond the purely temporal. Herein consists the element of transcendence in music. The relevance of a cosmological perspective is justified in so far as sound is the all-pervading cosmic phenomenon.

The universe of the musician may thus be described as more refined, more enriched, more purified than that of our own. It is the universe where the conventional laws of space, time and causality become inoperative.

What operates is the fundamental law of the intrinsic necessity of human being as being, the law (if at all) of self-realization. It is beyond all empirical laws.

Music is an unending quest, the eternal pilgrimage of man. The man in the musician is his music; the music of the man is his freedom, his transcendence, his spiritualism. Musicians are the pilgrims inspired by the message of and dedicated to their homage to the Infinite. The musician is thus far above the limitations of any caste, creed and religion.

Music is the *unique* Existence which is behind and above all laws; it is the unique *dynamic Moment* where the past is caught up and the future is got up. It is the *Essence* where the Divine and the human creation come very near each other; it is the struggle till we reach the depth of the heart and soul of things and beings. Music is and grows in the contemplation of the musician, and it is in contemplation that music yields back to him the feeling and willing of which it is an expression.

Music is thus the self-conscious principle of harmony which is transformed and transmuted in the transcendental unity within man which comprehends all the details of facts and events. In its negative aspect it may be said to be confined within the individual separateness; in its positive aspect it perpetually expands itself through a progressive march which melts into the vast ocean of dancing waves, the Infinite in man. Man is the music-maker, the dreamer of dreams, says Rabindranath. He adds: "It is for man to produce the music of the spirit with all the notes which he has in his psychology and which, through inattention or perversity, can easily be translated into a frightful noise. In music man is revealed and not in a noise."[8] Music is the eternal dream which goes across time weaving ceaseless patterns of Being and Existence behind and beyond all laws of natural creation. It emerges out of the tumult of profound bliss at the vision of Life in the infinity of human spirit. The musician is always aware of a continuum in his vision of life which transcends all boundaries of time, is devoid of all objects, is the expansion of the true present, is free from subjective-objective *conflict*. It is the musician who realises the man in him.

Music is a phenomenon which is a real-ideal object that exists, but exists nowhere. Its existence is always a potentiality of its being interpreted and reinterpreted by *Man*, the musician. It does have an existence because it interacts with human minds on the basis of human creativity. Music is the highest-level manifestation of the mind of the musician which lives in the musician's peace and tranquillity, the roads to human freedom, the roads to human communion with the ultimate cosmic principle—the vastness of the ocean of sound waves, the Infinity in Man. The expression of man in music is the beginning which melts away in his revelation where the musician gets merged in his own music and the distinction between the musician and his music is forever lost in a higher union, the underlying principle of unity being the cosmic phenomenon of sound in its refinement and purification created by the musician himself through his self-realization.

NOTES AND REFERENCES

1. Santayana, G.—*The Senses of Beauty*, p. 33.
2. Coomaraswamy has raised a very pertinent question. Why exhibit works of Art?
3. Sartre, J.P.— *Existentialism and Humanism*, p. 35.
4. It will be argued later on that for perfect and pure music the issue of the listener is a non-issue and the role of listener is absolutely superfluous in the context of pure musical creativity.
5. Sartre, J.P.—*Existentialism and Humanism*, p. 56.
6. The terms are borrowed from K.C. Bhattacharya—*Studies in Philosophy*. This issue will be taken up in connection with his analysis of *Rasa*.
7. *Studies in Philosophy*, Vol. I, pp. 355-356.
8. *The Religion of Man*, p. 80.

CHAPTER 5

MUSIC AND TRADITION

The musical tradition in India is technically called *Gharānā.* This is prevalent mostly in North India. Naturally *gharānā* has reference primarily to *Hindustāni* music. *Karnātic* music (which belongs to South India) does not appear to have any *gharānā.* So far as the salient feature of Indian music as a whole is concerned, one can safely say that it is based on oral tradition or the *guru-śiṣya paramparā.* No one can learn Indian music merely by following the text. As a matter of fact, any discipline whether intellectual or aesthetic or moral-sociological has, in so far as it is Indian, an intuitive basis and has to be learnt from a master having an intuitive vision.

In the process of learning there are three stages: *śravaṇa, manana* and *nidhidhyāsana.* The first relates to the factor of *learning* or hearing directly from the master (*guru*); the second, to the factor of *concentration* on what is thus learnt and the third, to *meditation* on the whole body of knowledge with a view to get oneself identified with it, where the subjective-objective process of human knowledge becomes properly anchored in the intrinsic vision of the learner. These three factors are typically the Indian way of learning anything.

Gharānā in the context of music basically means the rigorous pursuance of all these three factors by the disciple at the feet of his master. There is, therefore, no reason to suppose that in *Karnātic* music, this system of imparting lessons to the disciple is totally absent. However, in the history of Indian music, emphasis is on the presence of *gharānā* system in the context of *Hindustāni* music. Possibly some other terminology might be appropriate for the *Karnātic* counterpart. It will be a mistake to say that South Indian music has no tradition and is purely individualistic both in origin and development.

Gharānā literally means a particular musical tradition belonging to a family for a specific period of time. The musical tradition is concerned mainly with the interpretation of a *rāga* (the basic melodic pattern) and the style of its presentation. The family referred to here includes reference both to the direct descendants and to the disciples coming from outside the family. In their origin most of the *gharānās* were confined to the direct descendants only. One may, however, reformulate the interpretation of *gharānā* or musical tradition as follows:

Gharānā represents a school of performing music belonging to a house or a family at a particular period having its influence at least on three successive generations from father to son or from *guru* to *śiṣya*.

The number of generations as mentioned above may be said to have been arbitrarily fixed with no convincing reason in the background. The idea is perhaps that a particular style of presentation of performing music cannot be worth being designated as creating a tradition unless it continues for at least three generations. But the main point seems to concern the *uniqueness, novelty* and *aesthetic embellishment* in performance resulting in the unquestionable appeal to whoever listens to such a style of presentation; this may determine the influence of that particular style on the cultural coverage of a society in a period or in the periods to come; this influence will spontaneously confer upon the style the status of a *gharānā* or a tradition. No musician can claim: "I have created a *gharānā*". This is absurd. After all, music is the performing response of man's creative impulse to the spontaneous call of the *real*. A supremely illumined soul with his own intuitive spark can create something the influence of which cannot be ignored by the society for many generations. And this is how tradition is born. If in explaining musical tradition we have to depend entirely on teaching-learning process of master and disciple, then there is the fear of an infinite regress; "who is the first teacher who was never a student?" would be the question left unanswered.

In previous pages we have distinguished three elements in the context of musical form which are: the element of personality, the element of style and the element of artistic creativity (or the quintessence in art). The continuous, ever growing process in musical tradition consists in the understood importance of the quintessence in art in music along with the element of style relevant to, because accepted or recognised by, a particular socio-cultural community of a period and also with the element of personality.

Let us make the point clear. The element of personality and that of style are normally said to operate together, and such operation gives rise to many specific forms of music which in spite of some major differences in concrete cases of presentation may be located to be so organically related that they can be classified under some fundamental *gharānā*. But the *gharānā* or the tradition is to be characterized chiefly by the element of quintessence in art, the intuitive creativity of the great master which to some extent may be said to determine the elements of style and personality.

Thus *gharānā* or musical tradition may be said to have two aspects: *Nāyaki* and *Gāyaki*. The former is concerned with what the disciple directly learns from his master, the pure art form, its essence which the *guru* intuitively realises within himself without any training; the latter is concerned with how the disciple expresses his training through actual performance with style and personality blended together which in course of time gradually develops into an accepted style of presentation by a community of disciple-musicians which is normally said to be the representative of a particular *gharānā* or musical tradition of a period. In the stage of *gāyaki*, the three factors of *śravaṇa, manana* and *nidhidhyāsana* must invariably be at work; otherwise the basic Indian character of music would be lost.

Nāyaki of a *gharānā* may thus be said to roughly correspond to the essence of music as an art form which is the *hidden treasure* of the great master and the *gāyaki* of a *gharānā* may be said to roughly correspond to the elements of style and personality which are the *open treasures* of the disciples—may be the son of the master or a disciple who is not a direct descendant. The so-called open treasures may also have some element of hiddenness as resulting from the individual realization of one's own intrinsic sympathy *with* particular melodic patterns manifested in a variety of musical forms. But whatever be the character of openness or of the element of secrecy associated with it, *gāyaki* may be said to be rooted in *nāyaki*, and both together constitute what may be called a *gharānā* or a musical tradition.

The most notable feature of a musical tradition is its incentive to awaken the disciple's dormant abilities into fruitful artistic creations which in their turn will inspire thousands of others coming in contact with such creations either as listeners or as fellow-members of the same tradition or even incidentally as members of a society of the current period. In ancient period, when music was confined to devotionally based ritualistic practices of worship of deities, there was no concept of *gharānā*. Each musician had his own realization of music and created music according to the demands of his own realization without any adherence to any systematic learning.

The birth of *gharānā* can be traced to the mediaeval period (nearly about late 15th century) under the patronage of *Rājā Mānsingh Tomār* of *Gwāliar* which was further nourished and encouraged by the Emperor *Akbar, the Great.* By that time music in India was already under the revived sweeping influence of a new socio-cultural orientation. From temples and forests, from worship and prayer, it came to the Court of the Kings and Emperors for the purpose of entertainment. This is not all bad or derogatory; rather it has then become more accessible to the greater mass of the society who were otherwise deprived of this supreme divine gift of man. The vision of music and the musicians thus attains a new opening, and a new horizon is revealed to all; the vision may be new, but the view remains old. Music, in spite of minor change in the style of presentation, becomes the same in so far as it continued to be the outcome of the same spiritual realization from within. The new perspective of performing music becomes different though the inner *text* remains almost the same. It is hospitable to all because it has the wealth which is its own. It carries "its special criterion of excellence within itself and is practised in conformity with a rhetoric manufactured by those who are not in the secret of the subtle mysteries of creation, who want to simplify through their academic code of law that which is absolutely simple through its spontaneity."[1]

We have already said that music is a dynamic, progressive phenomenon which grows with the growth of life. It belongs "to the procession of life making constant adjustment with surprises, exploring unknown shrines of reality along its path of pilgrimage to a future which is as different from the past as the tree from the seed."[2] Thus from temple to court the transition of music is not to be condemned; rather it was necessitated by the inherent dynamism of music itself and the growing cultural needs of man.

It is in this progressive venture of experiments with new perspectives that new dimensions of music naturally emerge and help the case of music to grow further. In the same way, great disciples of music emerge under great masters and this gives birth to *gharānā* or a musical tradition. Such a tradition lives for a period in history in so far as it satisfies the socio-cultural needs of the particular period of history which is upheld and kept alive by what is already described as the *guru-sisya-paramparā.*

In such a musical tradition the disciple has to learn from his master and follow the lessons rigorously by making him free from all his psychological inhibitions and other so-called material obstacles in order to do justice to the lessons received from the master. But at the same time, the disciple may ignore the distinction beween recognised and unrecognised conventions regarding the style of presentation. He has to follow his own inner life, his own understanding and realization, his own commitment and the resultant approach to music which he feels compelled to adhere to and express through his chosen medium. These are the intrinsic laws of inner artistic necessity. The disciple may safely employ his own *style* either approved or forbidden by his fellow disciples or his contemporaries. In music all means of approach are sacred and noble provided they fulfil the demands of pure art and self-realization through a spiritual vision. Nothing is permanently forbidden.

The importance of *gharānā* in the context of music as a performing art consists in the intuitive discovery of and the consequent note combinations embodied in the so-called *Bandish* (the specific structural pattern of sequence of unique note combinations as the chief dominating feature of a total melodic pattern or *Rāga*) and the consistent sequential note combinations of ascending or descending order or both for a faithful narration of any specific melody together with some secret guidelines of emphasis upon any particular note or notes according to the sentiment or mood characteristic of the chosen melody. The master is accepted as the founder of a *gharānā* because of his supreme intuitive power of realization of music and his superb skill in rendering his realization in performance which he does not require to borrow from any master. Such intuitive realizations as spontaneously manifested through the dictates of the creative impulse within an artistic boundary are what constitute the genesis of a *gharānā,* and it is this which the disciples have to follow with unfailing obedience and a sort of ascetic involvement at the initial stage. After a long practice, he is able with the help of his own realization to infuse new dimensions of artistic creativity and thus the tradition comes into being, grows and develops with the secret code of laws which are laws imposed not from outside but from within the tradition. The sort of secret code of laws is presumably prescribed by the master himself according to the respective musical sensitivity of his disciples. In course of time such traditions become the standard style of performance of music and are universally accepted within a socio-cultural framework.

There should, however, be an *openness* in any tradition or *gharānā* for its further development, enrichment and refinement; otherwise there is the danger of its being stagnant or even lost or dead in some near future. The death would be welcome only if it gives birth to a richer new. It is clear that such musical traditions encourage not *imitation*, but *adaptation* of the basic lessons of music, so that it can grow with its own inner movement of growth. If music is all imitation then it is anything but music. Assimilation, adaptation and novelty are presumably the three major requirements of any *gharānā.*

Traditions in Indian music are thus always *oral traditions* with an understood reference to the intuitive realization of the master from where it starts. It is in this context that *gharānā* helps the transfer and transformation of the wealth of music from the master to the disciple. It is never to be interpreted as a closed-door institution; rather it is a two-way process. It has an *entry* and an *exit*, as we have pointed out earlier. The disciple is *initiated* by the *guru*, and after a course of rigorous training which varies in respective cases, the *guru* decides when the disciple can have an independent status of a performing musician. He encourages the disciple to cultivate music along with his own musical imagination, insight and indeed with his own realization. The tradition is characterized by the principle of the survival of the fittest subject to a verdict of artistic creativity acceptable by the present socio-cultural perspectives.

Indian music is never and had never been a happy-go-like device of human values. It is always sacred, noble and pure. It is never a servant of purely subjective choice and whims. So some reference to *gharānā* should be there for a proper cultivation of music according to the needs of society and culture on the one hand and on the other the intrinsic needs of one's own spiritual vision. Thus the tradition or the *gharānā* is worth the name which helps the current to flow. It is open where the current flows onwards and at the same time it guards itself if there is any possible danger of deviation amounting to distortion. It is like a flowing stream which fertilises the soil; it helps the growing life of man and enriches the life by adding new dimensions of vitality in values.

Musical tradition is not like a *lavishly splendoured pillar* which stands erect in its fullness, but helplessly depends on the lonely eternity of vanished years with a painful sense of vanity in its lost aristocracy. It is a continuous process of development which modestly discourages allurements of rash adventures and at the same time piously encourages new ventures for the enrichment and expansion of the musical horizon maintaining its purity and sanctity.

In developing his point, Rabindranath gives a very illuminating example. He argues that the bee's life in its channel of habit has no opening. It moves round within its narrow cycle of perfection. But the life of music has its time-honoured institutions which are *gharānās* having their own organized methods of perfection. When such institutions act as enclosures, then the result may be perfect like the bee's nest of wonderful precision. But then these would be unsuitable for the musical mind which is rich with unlimited possibilities of progressive perfection. Rabindranath[3] would painfully argue that if *gharānā* or the musical tradition remains confined to a handful of specialists who nourish it with delicate attention and feel proud of the ancient flavour of its *aristocratic exclusiveness*, then it is not a tradition in the desirable sense of the term particularly in the context of music; it would be like a rare wine stored in a dark cellar underground acquiring a special stimulation through its "artificially nurtured, barren antiquity". It is here that the human mind is helplessly flogged by a blindly possessive ghost of the past. Music has to come out of such cruel and destructive traditions. All traditional structures of music must have a sufficient degree of flexibility and elasticity so that they can respond to and receive from the immense variety of the impulses of life in its ceaseless forms of rhythmic growth. The so-called orthodox scriptures on music are of no avail in the growth of performing music as a creative art form. Rabindranath[4] says, very interestingly, that if *Nārada* and *Bharata*, after mutual consultation, can be said to have contributed the ultimate perfection of music to such a degree that we have only to obey and cannot create, then within such perfection, the essential character of music will be totally destroyed. Thus if the upholders of any *gharānā* do not make ample provision for the growth and pure creativity of music, then they would be good store-keepers, but do not deserve to be considered as real musicians. The role of musical tradition in maintaining the supreme cause of music is to see that music flows spontaneously for generations after generations not as blind repetitions, but as opening new horizons of the vast ineffable universe of music in the fullness of the spiritual life that man lives.

It may be noted here that of all the customarily accepted *gharānās* of music, the *Seni gharānā* (*Tānsen* as the progenitor) seems to be the most fundamental, while others are relatively off-shoots of the same. Thus we come across several musical traditions known and accepted as *Patiālā gharānā, Kirānā gharānā, Āgrā gharānā, Ātrāuli gharānā* and so on. It is rather difficult to construct a theoretical structure of the chief, distinctive features of any particular *gharānā*. A faithful chronology of *gharānās* is equally difficult to construct. It is also difficult to say emphatically whether *Tānsen* is the founder of Gwaliar *gharānā*, or there were some other great musicians before *Tānsen* who were the real founders of this *gharānā*, or whether long after *Tānsen* died some musicians having specialization in *Dhrupad or Kheyāl* form of music came forward and founded this *gharānā*.

Hindustāni classical music of North India can be traced to the reign of *Hārun-al-Rashid* (836 A.D.). It continued with the patronage of Kings and Emperors in subsequent times. In the reign of *Alāuddin Khilji, Baiju Bāwara* made his exceptionally remarkable stamp on *Hindustāni* music who first introduced the systematic singing of *Dhrupad*. Almost in the same period *Nāyak Gopāl* came to North India under invitation from the Emperor. He is said to belong to South India. The contribution of *Nāyak Gopāl* is undisputedly of great importance. We must refer to *Amir Khusru*, a Persian poet and a singer who, in the same period, flourished in India and gave a new shape to Indian music by a colourful blend of Indian and Persian style of music. This is said to culminate in the performance of *Tānsen*.

But according to some musicologists we have the first evidence of *Hindustāni* music in an articulated and a systematic form with definite melodic pattern in the lyrics of the Bengali poet *Jayadeva* who depicted the sporting play of *Lord Krishna* through a variety of musical themes.

The entire gamut of *Hindustāni* music, however, was completely driven to a new and richer direction by *Tānsen* under the patronage of *Rājā Mānsingh* of *Gwāliar* (1486-1516). After a gap of a period of about two hundred years of turmoil and cross-cultural rampage owing to political strategy of transfer of powers, *Rājā Mānsingh* with great effort and tenacity revived the pursuit and cultivation of Indian music; he was indebted to and inspired by his wife *Mriganayani* who equally was a great musician inspired by her own intuitive power of realization without receiving any formal training from any *guru*. It was in this period that *Rājā Mānsingh* invited *Tānsen* to his Court and gave him the highest honour as the greatest musician of India. The history of India's music will for ever remain indebted to *Rājā Mānsingh* and *Tānsen* for its survival and growth in richness. From *Tānsen* Indian music began to flow in a completely new direction covering almost all aspects of music as a performing art. *Tānsen* was mainly a *Dhrupad* singer; but he was equally expert in playing *Rabāb* and *Veenā*. He is said to have given lessons in both vocal and instrumental music to his wife who in course of time became the most worthy disciple of *Tānsen* at home. And *gharānā* is born here in the real sense of imparting lessons by a *guru* to the *śiṣya* whatever be the status of the latter. *Tānsen* and *Rājā Mānsingh* may be regarded as the pioneer in the field of Indian music, and almost all the subsequent schools of music together with their characteristic *gharānā* features may be said to have adapted one or other of the stylistic elements of presentation discovered by *Tānsen*. Among many *rāgas* or melodic patterns created by *Tānsen*, *Darbāri Kānādā*, *Miān-ki-Todi*, *Miān-ki-Malhār*, *Miān-ki-Sārang* are the few standard ones which are followed even today and with tremendous reception and appreciation from the common public, not merely from the connoisseurs. These are the *rāgas* which survived for several centuries and are still alive with their full richness of spiritual appeal even though the emphasis of rendering has been, in course of time, shifted from *Dhrupad* to *Kheyāl*.

From such a luminous history of Indian music which started from *Tānsen* one is inclined to draw the conclusion that all the so-called *gharānās* whether of vocal music or of instrumental music are off-shoots of *Seni-gharānā*, the word *Seni* referring to the name of *Tānsen* which literally means *king of Tānas*. This is the title which was reportedly conferred on him by the Emperor *Akbar* to whose court he was invited later on and settled permanently. His original name was *Rāmtanu*, the only living child of the father *Mukundarām Pande*. The *guru* from whom *Tānsen* received his initial training in music was *Swāmi Haridās* in *Vārānasi* and then in *Vrindāvana* who originally hailed from South India. The genuine Indian music with its ineffable spiritual undertone was thus born at places which are the sacred places of spiritual practices or *sādhanā*. *Tānsen* happened to be a gifted child with extraordinary musical talent lying dormant in him from his very childhood, because he was a *śrutidhara*, having the ability of instantaneously reproducing the exact tonality of whatever he heard.

It is normally accepted that the descendants of *Tānsen* are divided into two groups: the *Rabābiyās* and the *Veenkāras* in the field of instrumental music; in the field of vocal music all his descendants were equally competent with the required skill of performance and knowledge of the principal forms. Some descendants lived in *Rāmpur*, a state which was well-known for a number of centuries for its patronage to excellent group of musicians. *Tānsen* was a great *Dhrupad* singer, as we have said earlier, and *Rāmpur* was the home of some of his descendants who had expertise in his style of singing.[5] It would be an unpardonable offence to omit any reference to the *rāga Vilāskhāni Todi* which was created by *Vilāskhān*, the son of the celebrated *Tānsen*. The *rāga* is immensely popular even today because of its sentiment of *rolling pathos from one's within* and *in one's within*. The creation of such a *rāga* speaks of the exceptionally superb musical vision of the son because it was originally based on the basic scale of *Bhairavi* and not of *Todi*.

We do not propose to enter into a detailed discussion of the various standard *gharānās* of *Hindustāni* music, their distinctive features and so on, because such a task has already been done with great effort by Prof. M.R. Gautam in his book entitled *The Musical Heritage of India*. He has taken into consideration *gharānās* like *Qāwwal Bāche*, *Ātrāuli*, *Gwāliar*, *Āgrā*, *Sahāranpur*, *Sāhāsvan*, *Delhi*, *Fatehpur Sikri*, *Khurjā*, *Jaipur*, *Bhendi Bāzār*, *Kirānā*, and *Rāmpur*. These are the standard *gharānās*, no doubt; but one may be inclined to feel that some important *gharānās* have been left out; for example, *Gayā*, *Bishnupur*, *Betiyā*,

Indore, Patiālā and so on. Moreover he has taken into consideration those *gharānās* in greater details where the form of music cultivated is mostly vocal and mainly perhaps in the *Kheyāl* composition. There are *gharānās* where instrumental music was cultivated, and *Delhi gharānā* is particularly famous for the inventions of various rhythmic patterns on percussion instrument (*Tablā*). Hence, this is not an exhaustive treatment of *gharānās* in Indian music which has different aspects of expression in a variety of medium. That due importance was not given to the cultivation of instrumental music is evident from the list which he has prepared concerning the distinctive features of the chosen *gharānās*. All these features can be said to primarily belong to vocal music. Again, the treatment of some *gharānās* has an abrupt end where the distinctive features have not been explicitly stated. It is, however, interesting to note that maximum number of pages has been devoted to *Āgrā gharānā*; and minimum to *Rāmpur gharānā*; but inquisitive readers may expect the maximum about *Gwāliar gharānā* and also about *Rāmpur gharānā* perhaps on reasonable and legitimate grounds. The question still remains: whether the distinctive features or the main characteristics of a *gharānā* as listed by Prof. Gautam apply to *Dhrupad* or to *Kheyāl* or to both. It is a preliminary point that *Dhrupad* and *Kheyāl* cannot have the same characteristic features of presentation because of the obvious distinction of the musical approach in the respective cases.

One may further argue that there are some overlapping aspects in the list of the essential characteristic features. For example, the feature of "The sustained articulation of the *ākāra*, the vowel ā" is listed in connection with *Ātrāuli gharānā* (no. 1) and in a different terminology also in *Gwāliar gharānā* (no. 3). There may indeed be some common features practised in more than one *gharānā*; but the question remains: Do the other *gharānās* purposively abandon the *ālapa* with *ākāra*? The issue could have been made clear.

Again, mention is there about "distinct command over *tāla* and *laya*" as one of the main characteristics of *Ātrāuli gharānā*. Again the question comes: Do other *gharānās* lack the distinctive command over *tāla* and *laya*? It is rather risky to take the course of an affirmative answer which is perhaps warranted by the treatment of special features of *gharānās* as done by Prof. Gautam. Command over *tāla* and *laya* in a distinctive way is an essential feature of all *gharānās* because of their basic role in music.

With so many pages on *Āgrā gharānā*, most of which contain unnecessary personal details, there is no list of the main characteristics of this *gharānā*. Some other *gharānās* have also met with such tragic fate. Moreover, *Indore gharānā* has an exceptional character of giving birth to eminent vocal musicians even though it is said to have been rooted in some rather unknown instrumental musicians on *Sārangi*. Therefore it deserves a special treatment; but whether it has an independent status of a *gharānā* is indeed a debatable issue and cannot be set aside so easily.

The inclusion of *Ustād Amir Khān* under *Kirānā gharānā* may arouse some controversy. Some musicologists would prefer to include him under *Indore gharānā* (which for them has an independent status of a *gharānā*). The style of presentation by *Ustād Abdul Karim Khān* and by *Ustād Amir Khān* are vastly different; according to these musicologists there could not be any comparison at all except the simple fact that both are vocal musicians. Therefore, the inclusion of both these musicians under *Kirānā gharānā* may appear to be unjustified. Again, the inclusion of *Ustād Ali Akbar Khān, Pandit Ravi Shankar, Pandit Nikhil Banerjee* under *Kirānā gharānā* is definitely misleading. It seems that the author has treated this *gharānā* not with the requisite care and seriousness. These instrumentalists would have preferred to have been included under *Māihār gharānā* founded by the most versatile musician of the present days, *Late Ustād Bābā Alāuddin Khān Sāhib*. I had many occasions to talk to *late Nikhil Banerjee* and *Ustād Ali Akbar Khān* and I have strong reasons to believe that they would not accept the interpretation as furnished by Prof. Gautam. Moreover, whether *Ustād Amir Khān* "followed the style of *Ustād Abdul Wāhid Khān*" is a matter of great controversy. More historical details are necessary to establish this point specifically with reference to their personal styles of performance. Such a statement is rather hasty and is likely to create confusion.

The first point of the main features of *Kirānā gharānā* as listed by Prof. Gautam (singing in *sūr*) is present in all *gharānās*. As a matter of fact, the most fundamental lesson in music consists in this, and no one can say that there is or can be any *gharānā* which is totally indifferent to this aspect. Similarly, the distinction drawn between *svara-ālāpa* and *rāga-ālāpa* is another risky point likely to create confusion. No musician belonging to *Kirānā gharānā* or musicians allegedly deriving their imagination from the essential features of this *gharānā* can possibly be identified who consciously concentrate on *svara-ālāpa* to the utter neglect of *rāga-ālāpa*. Any critical reader might readily react in trying to identify such a musician—at least none could be found from among the names listed by Prof. Gautam himself under this *gharānā*.

The point is that it is very difficult to construct a correct theoretical structure of any *gharānā*, because in music, as in every other form of art, everything originates in purely intuitive feeling and is spontaneously expressed through creative measures and techniques. Even if one attempts to formulate a general structure of a *gharānā* on the basis of the essential features of emphasis regarding the style of presentation, there always remains an additional something, the *artistic surplus* which constitutes the soul of a *gharānā*, and this is beyond any theoretical formulation. However, the so-called essential features may be regarded as helpful more in understanding or rather locating an eminent musician in his performance with reference to a *gharānā* than in understanding the intuitively basic energizing force of the *gharānā* itself. Moreover, a disciple musician has always the freedom of deviation without distortion and thus the so-called essential features may be said to have only a surface value. It also happens sometimes that the same musician belonging to the same *gharānā* totally changes his style of presentation after one or two decades. Music is always a matter of growth, one of transformation. Therefore, it is not expected that the musician in his whole life time will adhere to only a few basic principles of presentation rooted in his particular *gharānā*. Indeed the supreme responsibility of the master musician as the founder of any *gharānā* is to see that his disciple have the proper realization of the *rāga-rupa* and a proper command over perfect tonality of reproduction of notes accompanied by an equal command over *tāla* and *laya*. The techniques and the basic styles should not be *too restrictive* and *all prescriptive*, and the disciples in being faithful to their own realisation can and should introduce minor (or in some cases major) stylistic improvements upon what was initially prescribed by the *guru*. To insist too much upon the so-called essential features of a *gharānā* is to obstruct the growth of music and to close the doors of the emergence of new master musicians from among the disciples. Thus any theoretical treatment of a *gharānā* with the purpose of concluding with its basic features appears to be self-contradictory in the universe of music which is an ever-growing phenomenon, unfolding and enfolding.

Karnātic music is comparatively on the safe side in not making too much of the so-called *gharānā* system as we find in *Hindustāni* music. The main outlook of the *gharānā* system should be to ensure that the disciple goes beyond the master in excellence of performance either partially or totally ignoring the so-called peripheral basic features, however numerous or however initially essential these may be. As the best example one could perhaps refer to *Ustād Ali Akbar Khān* who has surpassed his father in performance; but the father was always proud of his son. The *openness* for further development and enrichment of music and the consequent style of presentation should be the key-concept of any musical tradition.

Some, if not all, of the *gharānās* as dealt with by Prof. Gautam have already become extinct. This is the danger we already foresaw; and the reason is perhaps too much of adherence to the so-called essential features of the *gharānās* concerned. In this context the observations of Rabindranath[6] are worth mentioning: In exchange for a freedom of movement which is the prerogative of vigorous youth, we may gain a static perfection of senility that has minted its wisdom into hard and rounded maxims. Unfortunately, there are those who believe it an advantage for a child to be able to borrow its grandparents' age and be spared the trouble and risk of growing and think that it is a sign of wealthy respectability for an artist lazily to cultivate a monotonously easy success by means of some hoarded patrimony of tradition. But at the same time Rabindranath warns us that we may go too far if we reject tradition altogether in the cultivation of music.

In distinguishing between Science and Art Rabindranath says that for science the maxim is *I know*; for art, the maxim is *I perceive*. He refers to the last lines of one of his poems which run thus:

Let me go and see the smile of his face
Let me go and offer him my garland of flowers
Let me go and tell him that his flute plays music in my heart.

The musician says the same thing always in different ways and offers the garland of different flowers of his self-realization. He has the task of re-creating what he learnt from his master and this is what the society demands from musicians as *creative artists* of the age. According to his own imagination and training the individual mind of the disciple musician has always the right and responsibility to recognize reality in some of its special aspects and it is in this sense that a tradition grows and lives. In music, traditions can never grow if the responsibility or the task of the disciple is only to follow blindly the essential features without trying to offer new essential features. The essence of music is inexhaustible, and it demands new forms of creations. No finality can be claimed regarding the output of any *gharānā*; this can be done only at the cost of its premature death.

"So let us take heart and make daring experiments, venture out into the open road in the face of all risks, go through experiences in the great world of human kind, defying unholy prohibitions preached by prudent little critics, laughing at them when in their tender solicitude for our safety they ask our artists to behave like good children and never to cross the threshold of their school-room."[7]

The musician may thus be regarded[8] as a solitary pilgrim who after some initial training walks alone among the multitude and continually assimilates various experiences which he re-creates within his own imagination, unclassifiable and uncatalogued.[9]

NOTES AND REFERENCES

1. *Rabindranath on Art and Aesthetics*, p. 67.
2. *Ibid.*
3. *Ibid.*
4. *Sangeet Chinta*, p. 57 (*translation mine*).
5. This account is borrowed from Birendra Kishore Roy Chowdhury—*Hindustāni Sangeete Tānsener Sthān*, p. 45.
6. *Rabindranath on Art and Aesthetics*, pp. 62-63.
7. *Op. cit.*, p. 60.
8. The view is borrowed from Rabindranath, *ibid.*
9. This is a revised version of a lecture delivered at a National Level Seminar organised by Prof. Dipali Nag at Sangeet Research Academy, Calcutta.

CHAPTER 6

THE CONCEPT OF TĀLA IN MUSIC

Tāla is a technical word customarily meaning a series of sounds which are produced on a percussion instrument covered by any animal skin (duly processed) with the help of striking by the palm. The percussion instruments are many in number, for example, *Dundubhi, Mridanga, Khol, Pākhawāj, Tablā (Cymbals, Bells) etc.* We do not propose to enter into the historical issue of the origin and development of the nature and specific purpose of these instruments; we choose to focus on the concept of *Tāla* with special reference to *Tablā*. The reason is obvious. In modern times *Tablā* happens to be the most popular and most widely used as the accompanying percussion instrument by the musicians of North India.

Tāla has a couple of functions: (a) to accompany music (whether vocal or instrumental) or dance, and (b) to express its own rhythmic embellishment independent of any melody or dance. Here also we prefer to focus on (a) as mentioned above, the reason being the same as before. When we speak of music in the context of *Tāla,* we have in mind classical Indian music as in vogue in North India or in short *Hindustāni* music. There are varieties of classical *Hindustāni* music, namely, *Dhrupad. Dhamār, Kheyāl, Tappā, Thumri* and so on (in the vocal side); in the side of instruments we have music as played on *Sitār, Sarode, Violin, Flute, Esrāj, Sehnāi* and so on. Our focus would be on *Kheyāl* and on any variety of instrumental music. Once again, the reason is the same as before.

Tāla in *Hindustāni* music is what is the most essential part without which performing music would be stale and prosaic. *Music without Tāla* may be roughly compared to *cooked food without salt.* Thus *Tāla* may be said to contribute beauty, grace and cadence to music. Not to speak of *Hindustāni* music in particular, *Tāla* is necessary to any variety of

Indian music and even to Western music. Rhythm, which is the keynote of music, is maintained through *Tāla*. In fact *Tāla* and rhythm go together and one is insignificant without the other. In Indian music *Tāla* has, broadly speaking, both the functions of *Nihśabda Kriyā* and *Saśabda Kriyā,* i.e., without manifested sound and with manifested sound respectively. The former is present when *ālāpa* is rendered by the musicians which has a fixed and definite rhythm of its own.

Centuries and centuries ago, *Tāla* was discussed by ancient musicologists who were saint musicians and their observations were recorded in various scriptures of antiquity. A detailed classification of *Tāla* including the major guidelines of different *Tālas* can be had from the standard books on musicology.* So we choose not to enter into that aspect of the issue. We rather propose to focus our attention to some controversial issues which appear to be in need of a satisfactory solution.

Rabindranath in his visionary outlook has observed that rhythm is the most fundamental element in any form of music. It is the movement generated and also regulated by measured application of beats with the help of any suitable percussion instrument. It is also the creative and generative impulse in the very heart of the musician. As long as the notes are isolated, they remain prosaic and do not give rise to any permanent feeling of reality within. But if they are put into a rhythmic pattern they immediately *vibrate into radiance*; and perhaps it is here that the concept of *Tāla* is conceived as the medium of expressing and augmenting rhythm of any piece of music through a systematic method which involves a fixed and definite *time-span* which, indeed, varies in respect of different *Tālas* according to the intrinsic demand of the nature and beauty of the rhythm which they are intended to express.

But it would be a gross mistake to consider *Tāla* as only *keeping time*. Each *Tāla* has a specific name and specific combination of *bols* (the technical language in which *Tālas* are expressed) in accordance with the time-span required to maintain a perfect harmony with the intrinsic character of the specific rhythm. The time-measure, however, works as the main guiding principle, but it is not constitutive of *Tāla*; it is rather a *regulative principle* which controls from the background the expression of a specific *Tāla*. To maintain the rhythm and to infuse *life* into music is, however, the main purpose of *Tāla*. Rhythm is spontaneous in any music, and the musician in performing music may unconsciously follow any particular *Tāla* which is suitable for his own creation in performing music. But when *Tāla* is expressed through any percussion instrument

---

*See *Sangeeta Ratnākara* by Śārangadeva.

by a specialist, say a percussionist, it is not always spontaneous in the same sense. There is always a tacit understanding at play between the musician and the percussionist, since both serve the purpose of rhythm; the medium is different. *Hindustāni* music or music in general thus becomes an integrated totality on the basis of the harmonious blending of *melody* and *Tāla*.

The word '*tāla*' is said to be derived from *Tāli* (which literally means *clapping with the palms*) and is customarily accepted as a spontaneous expression of joy and cheerfulness. But if it continues for some time, no matter how long or short the time span is, rhythm is expressed in so far as the intervals between the clappings follow a uniform time span. Herein lies the secret of rhythm, namely, maintenance of uniformity of the duration of beats as well as of the intervals in between. If the said uniformity is reproduced on a percussion instrument the result is known as *tāla* which is technically defined as the rhythmic pattern of various components set up within a definite framework. The various components are technically known as *Bol*. When *Tāla* is thus technically understood, the word '*tāli*' acquires a new significance. In this technical context *tāli* serves as the guiding principle to determine what is known as *Sam* as distinguished from what is known as *Khāli*. *Sam* appears to be the most fundamental concept in any *tāla* as understood in *Hindustāni* music. This is the only important beat with a stress which controls all the other beats coming under any specific *tāla* and it is here that the rhythmic cycle starts and it is here that it ends.

The concept of *tāli* gives rise to another important concept, namely, *mātrās* or the requisite number of beats of a *Tāla* which are accepted as uniformly measured *time units* constituting the entire life and vitality of a *Tāla*. Since it moves in a cycle, the life of a *tāla* is a case of perpetual rebirth; it rotates creating new unique and subtle compositional intricacies giving rise to increasingly graceful rhythmic embellishments. The total number of *mātrās* and the time span originally recommended keeping in view the requisite rhythm are always maintained. Herein lies the immense potentiality of *Tāla* which requires an unfathomable vision towards rhythmic excellence. The duration of *mātrās*, however, varies according to the tempo which is known as *laya*.

Each *Tāla* is composed according to various sentiments of human mind towards musical realization. It is the sentiment which predominates in fixing the number of *mātrās*, in determining the *laya*, and also in composing the language of the *Bols*. All these together contribute to the rhythm which is the main switch gear of a *Tāla*. Thus we have *Tritāla* with 16 *mātrās*, *Jhāptāla* with 10 *mātrās*, *Rupaktāla* with 7 *mātrās* and so on. It will be seen and is generally accepted that the number of *mātrās* and the *bols* differ in different *Tālas*, because each *Tāla* is chosen to suit any specific sentiment. Each *Tāla* according to the specific sentiment has its own language of *bols* spread over required number of *mātrās*.

Nature provides us with the first evidence of the presence of rhythm in the Universe. The rotation of day and night, the dancing waves of the sea, the rolling peaks of the mountains, one uniformly slanting upon another, and so on are the evidence of Natural rhythm. When we turn our attention to ourselves the same is the case. Our vital breath and along with it our heartbeats or our pulsebeats which follow a strict regularity in *appearing, disappearing* and *reappearing* suggest that we are born with a rhythm of our own, and the sense of such a rhythm is intrinsically human.

Rhythm in music is *perfect cadence* which involves a uniform progression from one note to another. The notion of *perfect cadence* is usually understood as the progression from the *dominant* to the *tonic*. Similarly a progression from *subdominant* to *tonic* is known as *plagal cadence*. Many other varieties of cadence can be referred to in connection particularly with Western music. But what is of special attention is that cadence is the harmonious progression and weaving of several musical sounds according to some definite principle.

In the context of *Tālavādya*, cadence is usually understood to have an ascending order known as *uthāna* which, in a sense, fixes the tonality of the specific *bols* in accordance with the temperament or sentiment of the music which it is meant to accompany, or which it is meant to reveal in case of solo performance. Descending cadence is, on the other hand, known as *Tehāi* where a particular composition ends. Whether ascending or descending, it always adds to the beauty of the specific music.

Tehāi, in fact, provides a sense of repose which is felt to be necessary for purposes of embellishment. It is a *three-time-repetition* of the same composition of *bols* ending in the *Sam* in perfect agreement with the musical phrase which it is meant to accompany and beautify in a unique technical manner. It is also used in solo performance normally after a certain insurgence of complicated *bol* patterns produced by the percussionist out of his own imagination.

Tāla thus gives to music a regular, ordered feeling, and even flow. It may also deliberately tend to deviate from the flow by introducing some exciting phrases and cross currents which in disrupting the regular flow increases the charm of the melody. Thus the role of *Tāla* in *Hindustāni* music may be described as introducing and establishing a fundamental rhythmic embellishment within a polyrhythmic structure. The expected disciplined sequence, however, is never disturbed.

Tāla is *Unity in Diversity,* and is usually a cyclic movement ending where it started from. But inside the cycle there are both *horizontal* and *vertical* dimensions keeping intact the number of *mātrās* recommended and the *laya* given. *Tāla* involves a harnessing of each component *bol* which has to be carefully controlled to the desired end without loss of the enhanced charm but at the same time within the conventional structure together with a considerable exactitude. The highly rigid method of presentation which gives its artistic value is necessary to maintain the exact and precise timing of the terminating point (*Sam*). The technique (*Bāj*) of presentation may differ from artist to artist.

Thus it can be said that *Tāla* is the flow of rhythm upon a percussion instrument which consists of regular periodicity of alternative tension and relaxation. In this course various complicated infrastructures are interwoven where a particular time pattern defined in terms of particular *bols* with specific intervals recurs systematically. The immensely intricate network of a vast variety of *bol* combinations within the specific framework of the number of *mātrās* and the given *laya* are what constitute the most significant role of *Tāla* as performed by a percussionist in accompanying a musician. Each is complementary to the other. The creativity in melody through the structure and dimension of a particular *Rāga* by the musician together with the creativity of the percussionist through the corroborating structure and sentiment of a particular *Tāla* produces the intended totality of *Hindustāni* music which is fully absorbing and ever-radiating in essence and spirit. Improvisation which is the key-concept of Indian music can be said to be as much applicable to *Tāla* as to melodic performance. It is that with which the percussionist creates an incessant flow of rhythmic pattern like the continuous waves of the ocean, their rise and fall, and their rest. The musical effect, thus, owes as much to the musician as to the percussionist.

The popular notion of *Tāla* as being derived from the first two letters of *Tāndava* dance of *Shiva* and of *Lāsya* dance of *Pārvati* cannot be very easily denied. Again, there is another popular view that *Tāla* is derived from *Tal* which refers to the basis or foundation of anything substantial. This view is also too difficult to ignore. The popular views apart, the musicologists agree that *Tāla* is the basic rhythmic support on any percussion instrument which is almost invariably used in any musical performance or in dance. The *Dhrupad* form of vocal music and the *Veenā* in instrumental music take the help of *Pākhawāj*, one of the important percussion instruments because of the immense sobriety of the tonal production of sound which is presumably in agreement with the sober temperament of the music performed. *Tablā*, another percussion instrument, is used mainly in *Kheyāl* form of vocal music and *Sitār, Sarode, Violin etc.*, in instrumental music, because of the rather cheerful and relatively less sober form of music performed.

In *Karnātic* music the percussion instruments used are entirely different and we do not propose to enter into this subject for the sake of relevance in so far as our main concern is the North Indian form of music or the *Hindustāni* music. The characters of the rhythmic patterns on percussion instruments in *Karnātic* music are equally entirely different.

It is clear that the two main pillars of Indian music are *Rāga* and *Tāla*, the former referring to the basic melodic pattern of music and the latter to the rhythmic pattern followed in rendering the music. Maintaining the rhythm in a fixed, logical and systematic measure is, however, the main purpose of *Tāla*.

The *Tāla* in Indian music has a *circular* dimension; whereas in Western music it has a *linear* dimension. In Western music, *Tāla* is not as complicated as it is in Indian music, because the former mostly follows a *free rhythm* of a uniform division of two beats or three beats.

Any piece of Indian music as unfolding a specific *rāga* is set to a specific *tāla* according to the sentiment of the *rāga*. The *tāla* helps the musician to improvise a vast network of complicated patterns of permissible notes which can be suitably expressed by a parallel complicated network permissible within the framework of a specific *tāla*. The accompanying *tāla* is chosen always in accordance with the chosen *rāga* by the musician.

Several factors are worth mentioning in understanding the total phenomenon of *Tāla*. These are:

(a) *Mātrā* which are the metrical accents of the beats; these may be called subdivisions;

(b) *Aṅga* or the bar, which is the special division of *mātrās* to be followed in the presentation;

(c) *Laya* which is the tempo, either slow or fast, according to the spirit of the art;

(d) *Tāli-Khāli-Sam* which are the prominent beats of which the third one is most important in determining the point of the rhythmic cycle of beginning and end; the second one is the *indicator* of the *Sam* and is customarily designated as the *waive* or *beat-off*; the first one is the regular beat proportion of the total rhythmic cycle, and is designated as the *clap*;

(e) *Thekā* which is the general language of the *tāla* designated by meaningless words, mostly *onomatopoeic* (sound echoing the sense); these consist of *bols* which are suggestive of the tonality of the specific sound production of the percussion instrument, and constitute the major theoretical structure of a *tāla*;

(f) *Jāti* which is the classificatory principle of different *tālas* according to the *mātrās*;

(g) *Bhāva* which refers to the sentiments themselves as embodied in the rendering of any *tāla*.

The following table may provide a bird's eye view of the factors involved in a *tāla*:

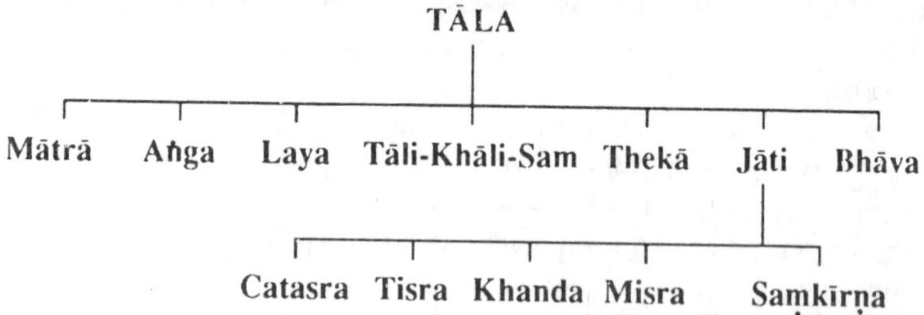

Let us now try to explain these factors serially.

Mātrās are always equally spaced with equal time length. Between the *mātrās* of a *tāla*, the time span should be exactly the same. This is a very important point in so far as perfect rhythmic effect is concerned. The nearest parallel is the heartbeat or the pulsebeat of a normal healthy person. The time span followed may be relative, may be equally short or equally long according as the tempo or the *laya*; but it must always remain the same in between the *mātrās* whatever be the speed of the movement chosen. Thus the duration of a single *mātrā* and the consequent duration of the time span in between the *mātrās* vary according to the *laya*. We have already noted the number of *mātrās* in connection with some important and popular *tālas*.

The question remains that the fixation of the number of *mātrās* in a given *tāla* may seem to be arbitrary. No satisfactory argument can be given in favour of such fixation. But the question may be roughly solved by referring to a man's own feeling and intention of how long a sentence with how many words in it he will choose to be able to fully express what he wants to say. There is no logic behind it. We can only say that for stylistic reasons and for elegance minimum words should be used for maximum expression. But nobody can dictate or decide about the number of minimum words in a given context with regard to a given subject of discourse. The matter has to be left to speaker-hearer context and the issue of elegance has to be settled by some other criterion. Similarly, in the context of *tāla* this much can be said that the number of *mātrās* has been intuitively fixed keeping in view the elegance of the rhythm which it seeks to convey which may be appreciated only by those who have an intuitive access to the aesthetic appeal of the total rhythmic pattern thus manifested.

Aṅga is the indication of the major division of the *mātrās* of a *tāla*. Not that every *tāla* follows the same *aṅga* or division of *mātrās*. Each *tāla*, according to the specific aesthetic needs, has its own division of *mātrās*. For example, *Tritāla* which consists of 16 *mātrās* has an equal *aṅga* of four each consisting of four *mātrās*; similarly *Dādrā* which consists of 6 *mātrās* has an equal *aṅga* of two each consisting of three *mātrās*. But the case is different with *Jhāptāla*. It consists of 10 *mātrās*; but the *aṅga* is imposed not in any conspicuously uniform order. The *mātrās* are divided into two basic *aṅgas* each of which consists of a further *aṅga* of two plus three. This will be as follows:

1 2	3 4 5	6 7	8 9 10
(a)		(b)	

In this way, other *tālas* have more complicated *aṅgas* for the requisite division of their constituting *mātrās*.

The question of arbitrariness may also be raised here; but the reply in solving this will be the same as before. No intellectual or logical argumentation is possible. The aesthetic intuition is the ultimate arbiter.

Tāli is what maintains the correctness of rhythmic progression with the help of a clap in a given *laya*. Its role is very significant in introducing discipline and smoothness by following the exact time-interval with nearly absolute precision. *Khāli* is normally indicated by a waive and it rests on that *mātrā* where sound is not produced as in *Tāli*; but it is not totally soundless, the silent gap. Its importance consists in its contrast to *Tāli* and is very significant in indicating the approximate arrival of the *Sam*. It is rather the *Sam*-indicator, indicating or pointing to the location of the *Sam* in the total cyclic span of a *tāla*. It is almost like a railway signal-bell of arrival and the departure of a particular train.

In different *tālas*, the positions of *Khāli* are located in different places. Not that it is always placed at the mid-point of the whole cycle. It has its own position in a definite *mātrā* which varies from one *tāla* to another. Thus in the most commonly used *Tritāla* the *Khāli* is on the 9th *mātrā*;

in *Jhāptāla* it is on the 6th *mātrā*; in *Kāhārwā* it is on the 5th *mātrā*. Again in *Ektāla* there are two positions of *Khāli*, one on the 3rd *mātrā*, the other on the 7th *mātrā*. This is when it is rendered as *dvimātric*; but when it is rendered as *trimātric*, there is only one *Khāli* which is located on the 7th *mātrā*. There are similar other cases.

The rather odd question appears again: Is the location of *Khāli* entirely arbitrary? The situation becomes worse when we come across *tālas* like *Tewrā* and *Rupak*. In the former there is no *Khāli*, and in the latter the *Sam* and the *Khāli* are both located on the first *mātrā*.

The whole matter seems puzzling and we have to depend again on the intuitive verdict of the saint musicians of the ancient periods who by their spiritual vision grasped the aesthetic musicality of the rhythmic pattern in diverse ways and did not feel the necessity of working out any reason. Perhaps any attempt at a rational reconstruction of aesthetic realization within one's own intuitive feeling is itself unwarranted, inasmuch as any number of surgical operations in search of *life* within a living organism may and will end in the destruction of life itself.

We may try to roughly explain the issue by referring to the grammar of punctuation. It is indeed a matter of one's own feeling where to put *commas* or *semicolons* or *fullstops*. In some cases, according to the cognitive needs of the speaker, a whole sentence may be constructed without any *comma* or any *parentheses*; the whole sentence runs with its intrinsic force and ends in the *fullstop*. In other cases, *commas* are used to distribute the emphasis of meaning which the given sentence is intended to convey. The change of the position of the 'comma' may change the meaning of the sentence; perhaps the change may be entirely to the contrary. No systematic grammatical rule can be followed for the use of punctuation in advanced literary and cognitive discourses. Similar might be the case with the location of *Khāli*, *Tāli* and *Sam* with no fixed grammatical rules.

Thekā is the accepted standardised form of a disciplined arrangement of different sound productions on percussion instruments attributed to suitable *tālas*. It is called the *mnemonic-composition*. Each *tāla* has its standard *Thekā* set to a particular arrangement of *mātrās* and their divisions, clearly indicating the positions of *Tāli*, *Khāli* and *Sam*. The *Thekā* is the simplest form in which any given *tāla* is translated into performance. *Dhā*, *Dhin*, *Nā*, *Tin*, *Tā* are the customary *mnemonics* used in designating particular *Thekās* each in its own unique pattern of sequential arrangement.

Jāti is a comparatively complicated concept in the *tāla* system of Indian music. It originally means a *class*. As we have already pointed out in the tabular diagram, there are five *jātis*, each including the respective *tālas* as follows:

(a) *Catasra Jāti* is said to include *tālas* like *Tritāla* (16 beats), *Tilwādā* (16 beats), *Chautāla* (12 beats) and *Kāhārwā* (8 beats);
(b) *Tisra Jāti* is said to include *tālas* like *Dādrā* (6 beats), *Khemtā* (6 beats), *Drut-Ektāla* (12 beats) and *Nasruk* (9 beats);
(c) *Khanda Jāti* is said to include *tālas* like *Jhāptāla* (10 beats), *Pustu* (5 beats);
(d) *Misra Jāti* is said to include *tālas* like *Deepchandi* (14 beats), *Rupak* (7 beats) and *Tewrā* (7 beats);
(e) *Saṃkīrṇa Jāti* is said to include the remaining *tālas* consisting of 11, 13 or 15 *mātrās*.

Again, we are confronted with a puzzling question: What is the basic principle of such classification? The answer, we confess, is very difficult to formulate because it will be seen that most of the popular *tālas* practised by the percussionists of the present days (for example, *tālas* like *Dhāmār, Adā Chautāla, Jhumrā* etc.) have been left out.

Some attempts, indeed, have been there to formulate the principle of classification which are as follows:

(a) *Catasra Jāti* deals with those *tālas* which have a straight order of progression;
(b) *Tisra Jāti* deals with those *tālas* which, instead of a straight order, follow the order of *Triple rhythm*;
(c) *Khanda Jāti* deals with those *tālas* which follow a *quintuple rhythm* of progression;
(d) *Misra Jāti* deals with those *tālas* which follow a *septuple rhythm* of movement;
(e) *Saṃkīrṇa Jāti* deals with those *tālas* which follow any sort of disciplined but complex rhythm which normally is accepted as *nonuple rhythm*.

Thus far, quite good. But the critics might say that the *tālas* which have been left out from the above list should have another item in the list of classification, otherwise they would be homeless. Or, should we have to accept that those *tālas* belong to a very low caste not worthy of being classified at all? Do they not follow any definite rhythmic pattern of progression? If so, how can they at all be regarded as *tāla*? It cannot be said that they have become obsolete and are not practised at all.[1]

The conclusion which obviously follows is that the classificatory principle is not sufficiently exhaustive. Perhaps the fact remains that a highly talented musician or a highly talented percussionist can with the help of his superb skill always, or according to aesthetic needs, change the rhythmic patterns of progression within the boundaries of any given *tāla*, thus infusing the rhythm normally meant for or prescribed for other *tālas* in accordance with the *Jāti* theory. The result is that the classification is not only non-exhaustive but is also non-exclusive. Inter-mixture of rhythmic patterns of progression is always permissible in *tablā* accompaniment in order to add to the beauty and elegance of the performance.[2]

As regards the *Bhāva* or sentiment of the *tālas*, it is customarily accepted that *Kāhārwā* or *Dādrā tālas* evoke romantic feelings, whereas *Chautāla, Dhāmār* etc. are *tālas* meant for the feelings of vigour or force. *Tritāla* is normally accepted as expressing the mood of peace or tranquillity.

Rabindranath, the most eminent musicologist and a creative musician of the present days, has taken a rather unconventional approach to the *tāla* system of *Hindustāni* music. He is not in favour of the supreme importance attributed to *Sam* by the traditional musicologists of the ancient days. *Sārangadeva* in his *Sangeeta Ratnākara* has perhaps given us for the first time a detailed and systematic account of the *tāla* system. The approach of Rabindranath can be treated as a revolutionary one in the sense that he has deliberately deviated (without distorting the fundamental spirit) from the rigid formulation of the basic components of the *tāla* system as conditioned by *Tāli, Khāli* and *Sam*. He feels that undue importance has been given to *Sam* and *Khāli* and he wants to make the *tāla* system free from such rigid obligatoriness.

Rabindranath has invented some *tāla* structures where there is no provision for any *Khāli* and consequently the importance of *Sam* disappears in these *tālas*. A few of such *tālas* are the following:

(1) *Jhampak* — 5 *mātrās*; 3-2 division; 2 *Tālis*; no *Khāli*

(2) *Jhampā* or *Ardha Jhāptāla* — 5 *mātrās*; 2-3 division; 2 *Tālis*; no *Khāli*

(3) *Ṣaṣthi* — 6 *mātrās*; 2-4 division; 3 *Tālis*; no *Khāli*

(4) *Rupakdā* — 8 *mātrās*; 3-2-3 division; 3 *Tālis*; no *Khāli*

(5) *Navatāla* — 9 *mātrās*; 3-2-2-2 division; 4 *Tālis*; no *Khāli*

(6) *Ekādasi* — 11 *mātrās*; 3-2-2-4 division; 4 *Tālis*; no *Khāli*

(7) *Navapancha* — 18 *mātrās*; 2-4-4-4-4 division; 5 *Tālis*; no *Khāli*.

There are few other *tāla* structures consisting of 10 *mātrās* or of 9 *mātrās* or even of 7 *mātrās* which were reportedly left untitled by the poet himself. Being a highly gifted poet, he also composes the lyric and has set the lyric into excellent and effective melodic patterns on the basis of the *tāla* structures created by himself. This is a rare example in the history of Indian music and musicology. I know not of any other exact parallel. References may be made to *Kāzi Nazrul Islām* and *Sri Atulprasad Sen* or even to *Nidhu Bābu* (Tappā); but they, in spite of their supreme artistic genius, cannot possibly be said to have gone above and beyond the depth of the artistic creativity of Rabindranath Tagore.

In undermining the importance of *Sam* in Indian music, Rabindranath has introduced a new dimension in the tradition of Indian music. Some critics have mistakenly interpreted this attempt of Rabindranath. They would like to hold the view that in his revolutionary approach Rabindranath has spoiled the Indian character of music and has taken it to the domain of Western music which is in favour of free rhythm. In other words, they are of opinion that under the influence of Western music Rabindranath has simplified the *tāla* system of Indian music with the result that such a system belongs neither to Indian music nor to Western music, and therefore has no artistic status of its own.

On closer analysis, it will be seen that the critics are entirely in a wrong track. In spite of the revolutionary approach, the new *tāla* system introduced by Rabindranath remains purely Indian in so far as it follows the *cyclic* dimension and not the linear dimension, the latter dominating Western music and the former dominating Indian music. Moreover, it will be seen that Rabindranath, as a faithful devotee of Indian classical music, has followed the typical *tālalipi*, the language (*Bol*) of Indian percussion instruments; he has also followed in strict measure the basic features of *mātrā, Aṅga, Laya, Thekā* and *Jāti*. The element of *Bhāva* or sentiment is obviously present because he himself composed the *tāla* structure which would, in all possible fitness of things, be perfectly suitable for the sentiment expressed by the lyric and the melody, both composed by himself. The *tālas* created by Rabindranath may be said to be classified under *Catasra Jāti*.

The poet seems to be influenced by the basic element of *artistic freedom* within some aesthetic boundaries. Freedom does not mean for him *free play* of rhythmic patterns without any principle of cadence. Perfect rhythmic balance and proportion are indeed very much there; the only fact is that he wants to remove the rather (which he seems to consider as) aesthetically superfluous character of the importance of *Sam* and consequently of *Khāli*. This, he fears, might obstruct the artistically spontaneous impulse and flow of the creativity of the musician. Under such a rigid *tāla* system with *Sam* as the chief dictator, the musician might always have a conscious tendency of coming back to *Sam* at any cost, and this might be harmful for the total creativity in music; under such a dominant dictator, the intended artistic depth of melody may not be fully revealed. On the other hand, the musician under such so-called mechanical lordship of the *Sam* might be inclined to some sort of exhibitionism of skill in correctly coming back to his lordship and surrender to his mechanical power, whereas he is expected to create a universe of aesthetic paradise with melodic embellishments. It is a sort of difficult exercise, says Rabindranath, like the difficult dance-performance of a woman with a vessel of water full to the brim on her head, but not a drop of water to overflow.[3]

The new unconventional *tālas* created by Rabindranath are, therefore, meant for the free, peaceful and relaxed mood of performance of the creative artist where he does not have to follow any strict, rigid maxim of correctly emphasising the *Sam*, and this is more in keeping with the typical Indian character of the spiritual vision in music which fosters the spontaneous revelation of the artistic treasures of the performer in accordance with his basic emotional appeal.[4]

NOTES AND REFERENCES

1. For the details of the *tāla* system in *Hindustāni* music and the various apparently arbitrary characters in its so-called theorization, I acknowledge my indebtedness to *Sri Jnanprakash Ghosh, Sri Sankar Ghosh, Sri Swapan Chowdhury, Sri Anindo Chatterjee* and *late Pandit T.L. Rana* who gave me some important suggestions which I have utilised here.
2. In this chapter I have mainly followed the analysis made by Nikhil Ghosh—*Fundamentals of Rāga and Tāla*.
3. This point has been further developed in the sequel.
4. This is a revised version of a lecture delivered at a national level Seminar organised by Prof. Sisirkona Dhar Chowdhury at Rabindra Bharati University, Calcutta.

CHAPTER 7

RĀGA AND RASA

Musicology as the science of Indian music is not a very popular study in present days. It may be compared to the state of Sanskrit language in India which, as a spoken language, is almost dead. It is confined only to the class rooms of collleges and universities.

Musicology is not practised in these days in the sense in which classical music can be said to be practised. Again, music may be said to be practised by persons who are more interested in *imitating* what has been learnt by them from their masters. The matter which really counts is *adaptation* and not *imitation. Creativity* which is the heart and soul of Indian music is lost in imitation. Rabindranath has made this point clear with the help of an autobiographical example. He refers to the case that once he got a letter from a person whose name he could not read out because of the bad hand-writing of the writer. But he had to give a reply to that letter. So in replying he used the name by exactly copying it as it appeared on the body of the letter. The reply must have reached the sender; but Rabindranath could not know the name of the person. Indian music under the strong tendency of imitation is close to the fate of mechanical reproduction without knowing a bit of what is being produced.

There is another kind of imitation in Indian music, a bit different from the above account. It can be said that a musician imitates music exactly as it is worked out in works on musicology with an understood reference to the grammatical nuances of a *rāga*, its *vādi* and *vivādi svara*, its ascending and descending note sequence etc. Such music is not real music in so far as it is grammar oriented. If any work of art is dominated by grammar alone, then the artistic dimension is likely to disappear; the whole thing would become dull and prosaic. The same is true of literature and of painting.

What is condemnable in Indian music is its over-emphasis on grammar, the so-called rigidity of formulation of a *rāga* structure and other allied injunctions found in various musicological treatises; what is equally condemnable is the urge for blind imitation. Grammar cannot give life to music or any object of art; it can, in the words of Rabindranath, produce a *mummy* which is far away from real artistic creativity. The beauty of a face does not consist in the anatomical description of the surgeon; nor does the beauty of a rose lie in the botanist's technical knowledge of flowers, their origin or their cytology and so on. Beauty depends on the depth of the totality of the elements concerned which is beyond the grasp of intellectual exercise of grammatical analysis or argumentation.

The creative musicians of India may follow the grammar of music only as the guiding factor at the initial stage; he may not even consciously follow the grammar as prescribed. A good work of art may be analysed into a grammatical structure after the work of art is done. Grammar, in this sense, can be said not to precede but to follow music.

But the question arises: What then is the specific task of the musicologist? Is he expected to create the grammar according to the works of musical creation by musicians of legendary fame, or is he expected to construct a grammar of music according to which the musicians have to create their artistic forms?

A musicologist is not just the grammarian of music; nor is he a music critic. Most of the music critics are influenced more by the grammar which is rather superficial than by the essence of music. The task of the musicologist is to construct in intelligible terms the essence of music and in so doing he can take the help of the most minimum grammatical tools as are indispensably required for unfolding the artistic essence of a particular *rāga*. Some ancient books on musicology can be found to have been devoted mostly to the construction of huge grammatical calculations. But they are necessary neither for *creating* music nor for *understanding* music. They are interesting only to those who want to read *intellect* into *emotion, construction* into *creation, anatomy* into a *living organism, parts* into the *whole, details* into the *totality, description* into the *ineffable.* Music, like other art forms, is to be viewed from the emphasis on the latter half of the above pairs and not on the former.

The essence of music as depicted through a particular *rāga* is basically ineffable. No amount of language or linguistic description can exhaustively reveal the essence of music. Whatever attempts can be made by the musicologists, there always remains something which is only to be *felt* and cannot be described. Still the musicologist in his task of systematic construction of the essence and structure of Indian music has to resort to a rough and working formulation of the *rāga* structure which is the keynote of Indian music. Music is there long before the musicologists, even in the ancient period—starting from *Bharata* or *Matanga* or *Sārangadeva*—have attempted a theoretical construction. It is in this sense that musicology in the Indian perspective has always been a post-mortem analysis. But musicology is not all grammar. Its main task, as we have seen before, is to work out the basic feeling and emotion (or even the will) which is the source of music, out of which music flows spontaneously. It is never the case that the Indian musicians in order to create music have to read the musicological text books. At certain periods of history some musicians have been identified as supreme masters in view of their creative genius, and in course of time, a *gharānā* has come into being. But these are rather accidental features and not the essential ones in the analysis of or in understanding Indian music in the true sense of the term.

Once more we are confronted with the fundamental question: What constitutes the essence of Indian music?

Music, as it is understood in India, is mainly the spontaneous outflow of basic human emotions in the form of melodic tunes. What cannot be otherwise communicated can be said through music. This is the supreme power of musical notes or *svaras* which place music at the top of the hierarchy of all artistic creations of the world. Rabindranath had been very outspoken on this point. He would argue that if a man is terribly under the pains of sorrow or grief, he is spontaneously in tears; his weeping or sobbing expresses the deep feeling of his sorrow within. This cannot be expressed if one just says: "I am under deep sorrow". Language fails to convey the real feeling as actual weeping does. Almost in a similar way music expresses the innermost feeling of man which cannot be verbally expressed, still less by resorting to grammatically loaded forms of expression in language.

For every *rāga* in Indian music there is some such emotional core-content in man's innermost feeling the depth of which he alone can realize. It is from such realization that music comes into an articulated form of expression through *svaras* or tones. The task of the Indian musicologist is precisely to formulate, as faithfully as possible, the inner feelings of the immensely vast domain of human emotions and will in the verbalised form of a *rāga* structure. The observations of Rabindranath can be constructed as follows:

> The feelings conveyed by the rising sun in the freshness of the awakening mind are faithfully depicted by the musicologists in the *rāga Bhairavi* and also those conveyed by the setting sun in the

tiring mind of human beings after the turmoil of the whole day are depicted by them in the *rāga Puravi*. It will be seen that in both these *rāgas* the emphasis has been put on *komal svaras*; but the musicologists are careful enough to see that in the former *rāga* the notes are so arranged that they convey the feeling of gradual unfolding of the musical notes and in the latter gradual enfolding of the notes. The high perfection of the intuitively based understanding of the musicologists of India consists in their proper realization of the spirit of any *rāga* which is self-certified by their theoretical formulation in the arrangement of the note sequences and in the treatment of the ascending and the descending order of the sequences concerned. The notes are so arranged and the teatment of the sequence of the notes is so formulated that in spite of the emphasis on *komal svaras* the respective feelings of morning and evening ,of the two different *rāgas* are clearly revealed to the connoisseur.

Mention in this context can also be made to the *rāgas Jaunpuri* and *Darbāri Kānāda* which have the same ascending and descending order of the same notes; but a slight difference in the treatment of the phrase consisting of *pa, dha* and *ni* and the emphasis on a specific *sruti* of *komal gāndhāra* with a little oscillation in *Darbāri Kānāda* make the respective appeals of the *rāgas* entirely different. Many other cases may be cited. The *rāgas Bhupāli* and *Deskāra* differ in the emphasis on a single note (*pa*, in case of the former and *dha* in case of the latter) while the notes and their order of ascendance and descendance remaining the same; similar is the case with *Ābhogi* and *Kalāvati* where the difference consists only in the change of scale in the given octave.[2] But the main point here is to show how immensely difficult the task of an Indian musicologist is and with how much responsibility and caution he has to formulate the basic *rāga* structure of Indian music keeping in view the specific emotive feeling which every *rāga* seeks to convey. The orientation is *wholly* spiritual and this alone enables the musicologist to dive deep into the core of Indian music. Grammar acts as a hindrance, a permanent stumbling block in the musicologists' supremely purified task of theoretical construction of Indian music. The most crucial point we are trying to arrive at is this: *Rāgas* existed with the musicians long before they are theorized or standardized by the musicologists and that the musicologists like the musicians are equally spiritually gifted, so far as Indian music is concerned, in their attempt at theorization or standardization, a task which can never be claimed to be complete or exhaustive because of the eternally new dimensions of appeal of human emotion and will. The *connection* between actual performing music and its so-called theoretical counterpart can only be intuitively grasped and not by, or perhaps never by, intellect. A musician may follow a particular *rāga* without consciously knowing its theory: it is the task of the musicologist to decide what particular *rāga* is under consideration by the musician. The musician's primary interest is and should be to give a shape to his inner feeling with the help of certain notes and their intrinsically imperative sequence and not to give shape to a particular *rāga* as theorized. To the latter category indeed belong those musicians who are relatively on a low scale of spiritual perfection. Music, according to Rabindranath, is the place where man can see himself through the depth of his own inner feeling; it is not the place for acrobatics or gymnastics. Those who indulge in latter in the name of music are to be condemned. Exhibitionism of skill in the name of music is to be denounced for ever.

The spiritual vision of the musician consists in his ineffable ability to spontaneously express his own feeling in its full-depth dimension which springs from his own realization of the inner self within; the spiritual vision of the musicologist consists in his ability to theorize performing music in articulated note patterns and sequences with all the finest nuances necessary for *artistic creativity*; the spiritual vision of the connoisseur consists in realizing the connection between the music as performed and its theoretical articulation. A hierarchy of spirituality has to be accepted where the musician as a pure, creative artist is at the top.

From another point of view, the music-connoisseurs may be brought under two groups: (a) performer and (b) listener. To the former group belong those musicians who, instead of creating music independently of the musicologists, follow the musicologists' standardization in performing music according to their own spiritual vision and intrinsic necessity of feeling. Such musicians have also the gifted power of creating music in the sense of developing the existing theorization done by the musicologists in greater and more subtle way; this opens a new and vast horizon of music on the basis of their own realisation accompanied by a rigorous and ascetic practice. To the latter group belong the listeners who can appreciate the musicians' creativity, but for some reason or rather are not able to create music. The former group of musicians in their continued and ceaseless pursuit of musical creativity may perhaps be said to give rise to what is characterized as the *guru-śiṣya-paramparā* in Indian music.

Thus we may, with some reservations, roughly distinguish between two kinds of musicians: To one group belong those musicians who create music in their performance in accordance with the guidelines as furnished in different musicological scriptures, and to the other group belong those musicians who create music in their performance as independent of any such scriptures. For the sake of convenience, the musicians belonging to the first group may be regarded as music-connoisseurs of a very high order having a profound spiritual vision, the scriptures only contributing to the fruition of their vision; the musicians belonging to the second group may be regarded as the highest order musicians giving us music as pure creativity independent of the scriptures which are only the theoretical formulations deriving the guideline from such creativity.

The role of music critics has no place in this scale of hierarchy because they make too much of theorization in music, perhaps more than the musicologists themselves have done. Their attitude towards music can be best compared to the attitude of the orthodox grammarian to a poem.

The renowned musicologists of India are many among whom the names of *Dattila, Nārada, Bharata, Matanga* and *Sārangadeva* deserve special mention because they have done the pioneering work on music. The other works on musicology may be treated as a sort of treatment which may be ultimately traced to these fundamental ones. Apart from cross-references, we are also acquainted with the works of *Viśvavasu, Kohala, Pārśadeva, Ahovala, Mammata, Kallinātha, Locana, Venkatamākhi* and others. It would be a gross injustice to say that these musicologists devoted only to the analysis of *rāga* structure. They handed over to us vast and extensive theories of Indian music covering the areas of *Rāga, Tāla, Rasa, Bhāva, Chhanda* and other allied issues.

The entire musical system of India has been analysed and theorized in a very firm and systematic manner by *Sārangadeva* for the first time. History is rather obscure as regards the musicians or the specimens of music which the musicologists derive their inspiration from. It may not be improper to maintain that they themselves were practising musicians and later on thought about the necessity of theorization of music. Actual music as a real art form must be there before its theorization, because in real art "theory does not precede practice but follows it. Everything at first is a matter of feeling. Even though the general structure may be formulated theoretically, there is still an additional something which constitutes the soul of creation. Any theoretical scheme will be lacking in the essential of creation—the internal desire for expression—which cannot be formulated. Despite the most accurate weights and balance to be had, a deductive weighing can never suffice. True proportions cannot be calculated, nor true scales be found ready-made. Proportions and scales are not outside the artist but within him; they are what we may call a feeling for boundaries, artistic tact—qualities which are innate and which may be raised by enthusiasm to genius."[3] Thus music is not so much according to the physical laws, nor according to theoretical injunctions as according to the laws of internal necessity which is the law of the soul, the spiritual realization of man. Theory in music provides a guideline, a tentative one in accordance with which one may proceed further in creation, but it is not all music in its creativity.

In constructing the theoretical framework of music, the musicologists should be careful enough in being faithful, as far as possible, to the inner self of the musician, his creative impulse, his intuition, his spiritual realization. If it is all mechanically formulated, then it will destroy music; it will even not be able to provide a guideline which is normally expected from the musicologists. A picture of the anatomical structure of a human body may be highly perfect, perhaps devoid of any error; but if it is claimed to be a complete picture, it will be seen that it fails in doing justice to the phenomenon of *life* in the human being. Again, some human beings may be born whose anatomical structure may deviate from the accepted standard ones; but it is quite possible that such human beings exhibit life more vigorously and rhythmically than those having a perfect anatomical counterpart. As a living man in the fullness of his life does not know how his anatomy works, so a real musician may not and perhaps does not know how his music can be theorized. Musicology is a *post mortem* analysis as human physiology basically is. But the analysis, how much grammatical orientation there may be as admissible, must do justice to the essence of the phenomenon concerned which is always beyond complete theorization. Attempts should indeed be there for better understanding of music or of life, but such attempts cannot create music or create life. Once a man knows his own anatomical structure, its merits or its demerits as they incidentally are in his case, he would be able to modulate the pattern of his living as a whole. Similarly the great benefit which a musician can derive, if at all, from his own interpretation of a musicological treatise is just to change or alter his style of performing music in order to ensure a richer creativity. Music is not born out of musicology as life is not born out of physiology. Music is not to be taken as in conformity to musicological rules; the real story is just the other way round. The foundations of Indian musicology may thus be said to be rooted in *seeing through* and not *looking at* the inner essence of music, its spiritual core-content.

Any discussion on the intuitive basis of Indian music would remain imperfect, if we do not pay proper attention to two fundamental concepts, one is the concept of *Rāga* and the other is the concept of *Rasa*. These are the two key-concepts of Indian music.

A *rāga* is normally understood as the basic melodic pattern whether simple or complex, consisting of several notes either five or six or seven, but not or perhaps never less than five, in a fixed ascending and descending order which may be the same or different (one ascending order and a different descending order). The progression of notes has a definite structure exhibiting a specific balance, harmony and proportion of the notes thus used. In most of the cases there is some uniqueness in the treatment of the notes, either a single note or a combination of two or three notes together. This is in keeping with the mood or sentiment of the *rāga* which it tends to depict.

The development of Indian music shows that the standard seven notes are discovered first and then some flat notes are discovered which are characterized as *Komala svaras*. These are *ri, gā, dha* and *ni*; with *ma* there is no flat note, but a sharp one which is characterized as *Teevra Madhyama*. Thus we have: *Sā, Ri-Ri, Gā-Gā, Ma-Ma, Pa, Dha-Dha, Ni-Ni* which end in *Sā* of the next upper octave. This picture includes *suddha* and *komal svaras* with the addition of *teevra madhyama*. Some *srutis* are also discovered which are minute and subtle subdivisions in between two major notes. There are twenty-two such *srutis* normally accepted as producing musical effects. Other possible subdivisions are rejected as being non-musical.

If we take *sā* as the starting point of our musical scale, then the picture of *śrutis* will be as follows:

sā	*ri*	*gā* :	*ma* :	*pa*	*dha*	*ni*
4	3	2	4	4	3	2 = 22

This is discovered by *Bharata* and is mentioned in his *Nātyaśāstra* as follows:

Sādjāscatusrutirgeya rishavastrisruti smrita
dvisrutiscapi gāndhāro madhyamasca catusruti
Catusruti pancama syāt trisrutidhaivata tathā
dvisrutistu naisādasyāt sadjāgrāme svarāntare.

In formulating a *rāga* structure or the melody pattern of Indian music due emphasis has to be given on some notes as *vādi, samvādi, vivādi* and *anuvādi* according to the standard principle of assonance and dissonance. This principle is related to the essential harmonic nature of the component notes constitutive of a specific *rāga*; in other words, the harmonic relationship between the component notes of a *rāga* structure which is an integral part of Indian music is closely connected with the notion of *vādi* and *samvādi* on the one hand and *vivādi* on the other, and this can be worked out according to the principle of assonance and dissonance. It has been seen that the assonance becomes most harmonic in respect of notes resting at a distance of eight and twelve *śruti* intervals.

The present day *rāga* concept owes its origin to *Bharata* in his analysis of *jātirāgas*, to *Matanga* in his distinction between *Desi* and *Mārga sangeet* and also to *Sārangadeva* in his detailed treatment of *rāga* in the historical perspective. The modern concept of *rāga* combines the fundamental points in the treatment of all these great musicologists and thus becomes a very clear and convincing concept enabling one to understand Indian music in its proper spirit.

Bharata mentions the term *rāga* as associated with another term *jāti* with the result that for him a *rāga* has always to be understood as a *jātirāga*. The reason for the emphasis on the predicate *jāti* in connection with *rāga* is not clear except for the fact that he mentions ten characteristics of *jāti* which may be of some relevance in understanding what a *rāga* is or should be.

The ten characteristics are:

(a) *graha*,
(b) *amṣa*,
(c) *tār*,
(d) *mandra*,
(e) *nyāsa*
(f) *apanyāsa*,
(g) *alpatva*,
(h) *bahutva*,
(i) *sādava, and*
(j) *audava.*

Jāti normally means a 'class'; but *Bharata* probably has in view the class-character or the essential quality manifested by the specific use of a *svara* in the context of a *rāga*. All these notions are well-accommodated in the modern concept of a *rāga*.

Bharata has further spoken of *suddha* and *vikrita jāti*; in the modern concept *rāgas* are classified into *suddha, salāga* and *saṃkirṇa*. The *vikrita jātis* originate from a combination or intermixture of several *suddha jātis*; similarly *samkirṇa rāga* of the modern period is understood to be a result of a harmonious blending of different *suddha rāgas* or of a *suddha* and a *salāga rāga*. *Suddha rāga*, as the term suggests, is *rāga* in its purest form which is entirely free from the influence of any other *rāga; salāga rāga* is a *rāga* which is a manifestation under the influence of another *rāga*. That new *rāgas* are being created even today is a matter beyond dispute; and in most such cases the influence of many *rāgas* can be discernible.

Matanga has emphasised the character of *colourfulness* in the context of a *rāga* and defines a *rāga* as that which adds colour to what is otherwise colourless. Apparently there is nothing exceptional in this definition. But the real significance of this definition lies in its emphatic reference to the role played by the *vādi svara* in a *rāga*. A *rāga* is worth the name only by the proper selection and use of the *vādi svara* which functions as the *king-note* of the *rāga* structure in achieving the essential quality and the aesthetic embellishment in conformity with the sentiment and mood to be depicted. The *samvādi svara* acts as the *minister-note* and *anuvādi svaras* act as *attendants*. Utmost care has to be taken regarding the *vivādi svara* which acts as the *enemy-note* and is to be avoided or is to be used as one treats his enemy in defeating him. The main idea behind this seems to be that a king becomes a king in the true sense of the term when he defeats his enemies. A king without any enemy being defeated is not a dignified king. Similarly in constructing a *rāga* structure the enemy-notes have to be selected and properly defeated so that the king-notes and other auxiliary notes stand in full glory and excellence.

In the modern concept of *rāga* all these aspects have been incorporated; we need not go into details regarding the observations of *Sārangadeva* on this point. It will be seen that the salient points of his observations have all been taken into account in the theoretical treatment of the *rāga* structure of the present day.

The important point in constructing a *rāga* structure seems to be the selection of the component notes and their unique order of sequence both in the ascending and the descending process (*calana*) together with a specific twist (technically called *pakad*) with regard to a particular phrase consisting of two or more notes according to the needs of the specific sentiment or mood. The most important point seems to be the selection of the *vādi* note first which is the dominant note in a *rāga*, and acts as the sonant, then the consonant note or the *samvādi*, then the assonant one or the *anuvādi* and lastly the dissonant note or the *vivādi*. All these notes evolve in relation to the dominant sonant note or the *vādi*. The *graha* is normally taken as the initial or the starting note of a *rāga*, and *amsa* is, broadly speaking, the same as *vādi*; the *nyāsa* is the note which conveys the idea of a note that concludes the note sequence of a *rāga* structure.

It is to be kept in mind that the selection of the dominant note is always a verdict of *intuition* and not of the *grammar* of music.

Now, to come to the other equally important aspect of Indian music closely connected with the concept of *rāga*, namely, the concept of *rasa*. *Rasa* is taken to be the vitalising or the energizing power of a *rāga*.

If *rāga* is the melodic core or microcosm of Indian music, *rasa* is its basic aesthetic appeal which enriches the *rāga* in the domain of art, and infuses life into music so that it grows and becomes an unending process flourishing in diverse forms of development culminating in spiritual enlightenment, a communion with the Infinite—the fullness in man. There can be no *rāga* without an accompanying *rasa*. This is perhaps the unique feature of Indian music which cannot be found in any other musical heritage.

It is indeed very difficult to find an exact English equivalent of the word *rasa* as it is understood in Indian aesthetics. The nearest so-called equivalent would be 'feeling par excellence' or 'the eternal value that is felt as an end in itself'. Such a feeling stands on a higher level as compared to other feelings which are directed to empirical phenomena. *Rasa* thus may be said to signify a feeling of enjoyment of which there is no direct empirical object; it is a sort of trans-empirical feeling inwardly directed. There may be an object which is incidentally there; but the object does not figure as a *fact* but as a *value*. K.C. Bhattacharya[5] proposes to consider *rasa* as a case of artistic enjoyment which is not glued down to any empirical object. He elaborates his point with the help of the following example:

"In sympathising with a child enjoying his toy, I am not interested like the child in the toy itself but in his enjoyment. Sympathy with joy is also joy but it is freer than the primary joy. I do not unconsciously project the joyous look or expression on the toy; I do not see it there like the child. I at best feel like imagining it."[6] He proceeds to develop his analysis of *rasa* as the artistic enjoyment by considering it to belong to a higher level of enjoyment than ordinary enjoyment. He holds that the beauty of an object does not appear to the artistic feeling as a quality or adjective of the object. He emphatically points out that *rasa* is that artistic enjoyment which is presented "as a floating or transcendent expression like that which is consciously *projected* by sympathy on the object of the feeling sympathised with."[7] This is why, he says, *rasa* or artistic enjoyment belongs to a higher level. It, in his opinion, belongs to the level of duplicated sympathy or *sympathy with sympathy*. *Rasa*, he argues, stands on a level higher than ordinary sympathy which again constitutes a level higher than primary object-feeling at the empirical level. In his own words, *rasa* can be regarded as that artistic or aesthetic enjoyment "which is not merely *free* from the entanglement of fact but as the *realization* of an eternal value, as an identification with the aesthetic essence without loss of freedom."[8]

Rasa thus can be said to consist of one's identification with the essence in the aesthetic enjoyment. This has a two-fold direction—the projective or creative direction and the assimilative or abstractive direction.[9] In the former, says, K.C. Bhattacharya, the feeling becomes objective but does not get entangled in the given fact. It transfigures the *fact* into an *eternal value*. In the latter, the feeling of detachment of the subject does not give rise to any feeling or unreality. The value or soul of the object is drawn out as it were and "reposefully enjoyed". He concludes: "In the former, there is freedom in spite of enjoying contact: and in the latter, enjoyment or reality in spite of detaching freedom."[10]

Rasa thus may be said to be rooted in the essence of feeling of the highest order. It is to be understood either as an eternal feeling or as an *eternal value as felt*. It involves some factors which distinguish it from the object which is its projection and often misleadingly gives rise to the idea of identification with the empirical object. These factors are: expression, detachment and eternity. These can be realised, though not necessarily, in the location of any given object only as the *projections* of *sympathetic feeling* together with *contemplative feeling* without loss of freedom. Its overall character is transcendental.

It is said that *Bharata* admits four *rasas* to be basic which are *Śringāra, Raudra, Vira* and *Bibhatsa*. There are four other *rasas* which are dependent on or derivative from these fundamental *rasas*. The derivative *rasas* are: *Hāsya, Karuṇa, Adbhuta* and *Bhayānaka*. According to some, there is a ninth one (called *Śānta rasa*) which is the highest of all *rasas* in the sense that at this stage man reaches his identification with a self-luminous spiritual joy where all other *rasas* coincide in a transformed and transmuted form.

Thus in standard literature on musicology we come across a total of nine *rasas* (eight plus one) which are as follows:

1. *Śringāra* or Love
2. *Karuṇā* or Grief
3. *Raudra* or Anger
4. *Vira* or Enthusiasm
5. *Bibhatsa* or Disgust
6. *Hāsya* or Mirth
7. *Adbhuta* or Wonder
8. *Bhayānaka* or Terror
9. *Śānta* or Peace / Tranquillity.

In elaborating the details of the list of *rasas* accepted by Indian musicologists we have to point out that each has its empirical counterpart which should not be emphasised when considered at the aesthetic level.

The *rasas* or the *artistic experiences* have been always interpreted from a trans-empirical point of view. In other words, the aesthetic level, by definition, transcends the empirical level, and the *rasas* as aesthetically eternal values transcend their ordinary psychological determinants.

To take the case of Love. The empirical emotion of love consists in the mutual interaction between a man and a woman which is inclined mostly to the physical level. It is rather temporary in the sense that it lasts so long as the state of infatuation continues. In aesthetic level, on the other hand, it is permanent, an eternal value where there is no question of a male body or a female body. The individuality of the loving persons (as in the case of empirical love) disappears; what remains, as it were, is a *situation* which is inspiring and absorbing, and the result is a pure delightful state of highest level love which has no physical counterpart. It may, at best, be treated as the artistic enjoyment of unity which emerges as a consequence of the merging of two embodied selves (and not two bodies) into one higher self. According to some critics, the nearest equivalent in understanding the real significance of love as a *rasa* or an aesthetic enjoyment is the divine love of *Rādhā* and *Krishna* (as depicted in *Geeta Govinda* by *Jayadeva*).

Still, it may be argued that such a reference to the union of two selves is not even necessary. One can have the unique experience of *love* in any object of nature which arouses in him the inescapable emotion of being inspired by and getting absorbed in the higher level appeal which it embodies.

Similarly, in every other case it may be shown that the *rasas* belong to a trans-empirical level and should not be treated as confined to gross empirical facts or situations. *Karuṇa* or sorrow or grief has been exemplified in its proper spirit as a *rasa* by *Kālidāsa* in his *Meghadutam.* In like manner, *Adbhuta rasa* has been exemplified by *Bhavabhuti* in his *Uttararāma Caritam.* In connection with terror as an artistic enjoyment one may refer to the feeling of *Dushyanta* at the sight of fleeting deer. As illustrations of *Raudra rasa* one may refer to the aesthetic experience of *Asvatthama* or *Parasurama.* In this way, all the *rasas* can be separately shown to signify a spiritual state of human beings which transcends all empirical limitations or boundaries. The *rasas* are universal since there is no limit or restrictions to whatever is transcendent. Every person potentially has an access to such artistic enjoyments.

Of all the *rasas, Śānta rasa* appears to be most illuminating since it happens to be of supreme importance. The human mind at this level is in a state of pure joy where all other states are in perfect equilibrium and the mind enjoys pure bliss where all distinctions or individuations are lost or fused into a luminous whole self-radiating and all-encompassing. It is rather mysterious that *Bharata* did not mention this *rasa*.

We now propose to enter into a very controversial aspect of Indian musicology, namely, the relation between *rāga* and *rasa*.

It is normally accepted that a *rāga* is something more than its mere melodic pattern or the melodic microcosm; it has something more than its sonal structure which is, as it were, its body. It has a soul which inhabits the body. Such a conception is warranted by the simple fact that a *rāga* has never been interpreted as something stagnant; it always grows like a living organism. History bears ample evidence for such a conception. The *soul* of a *rāga* is the *rasa*, the indwelling spirit. A proper assimilation of a *rāga* with its inherent *rasa* is highly intuitive and no amount of logical or grammatical calculation can establish the authenticity of such assimilation. The matter is and should be life, as we have already indicated, to the verdict of intuition based on deep meditation (*dhyāna*); one has to wait to see how deeply it affects any particular socio-cultural framework in a given period of history in man's eternal quest to discover the true, real man within him. In the cases of genius, the factor of deep meditation may appear to be redundant.

It is now perhaps clear that each *rāga* in Indian music is associated with a definite *rasa*. In other words, *rāgas* are understood as the musical vehicle to convey a specific aesthetic-cum-emotional sentiment characteristic of a *rasa*, its definite ethos, its spiritual and trans-empirical appeal. It is this emotive-aesthetic principle, the indwelling or presiding sentiment which the musician tries to invoke with the help of a unique combination of notes, customarily called the *rāga*. The notes themselves have an intrinsic aesthetic value, each having its own artistic dimension as visualised by the great sages of India or the musicians of absolute dedication, the *sangeet sādhakas* or the *sangeet rishis*. In other words, particular notes (*svaras*) have been regarded each as having the unique character of giving shape to a particular *rasa*, each note signifying its own *rasa* appeal.

The proper interpretation of the *rasa* as dominating a particular *svara* requires a spiritual vision and consequent realization of the totality of the phenomenon of music. An untrained musician or a musician having no spiritual vision is liable to distort the musical phenomenon as well as the *rasa* behind. In this context Prof. O.C. Gangoly draws our attention to a very relevant analysis which refers to the reportedly musical practices of *Nārada* at his early stage. He observes: During his early practices of the science, when Kṛṣṇa wished to convince him that the former's musical practices had not yet given him the necessary technical perfection, "Nārada was taken to a celestial region where he found several wounded nymphs and angels, weeping in great misery, for, their limbs had been distorted and mangled. When Nārada enquired of the reason of the pitiable plight of the nymphs,—he was informed that they were the melodies (rāgas and rāginis) whose limbs have been broken by Nārada's unskilful attempt to render their true and accurate forms, in the course of his clumsy practices." He further adds: "The suggestion was that if one desires to invoke the spirit of the rāginis to descend from their celestial abode and live in their physical sound-forms, the latter must be delineated with loving tenderness, scrupulous care, reverence and devotion,—with all the accuracy of technical performance, as well as of spiritual vision."[11]

Apart from the mythological undertone of the above episode, there is an element of richer truth beneath. Man, at the earliest dawn of civilization, is prone to identify several Gods and Goddesses out of his helplessness against the powerful forces of Nature. Thus in regard to the natural forces of storm or rain or fire there is believed to be one or other God in the celestial region controlling such natural phenomena from above. Most of the so-called religious rites and ceremonials were intended to please the Gods or the Deities (according as they are associated as the dominant supreme power with one or other of the various natural forces) in order to get rid of the evils which such natural forces produce on earth and on the living beings. Thus came the Gods of the sky, like *Mitra* and *Varuna*; the Gods of the mid-air, like *Indra* and *Marut*; the Gods of the earth, like *Agni* and *Soma*. Of all the Gods *Indra* and *Varuna* happened to be most powerful because they were associated with those natural phenomena regarding which man thought himself to be most helpless. Gradually, this kind of polytheistic approach was superseded by a henotheistic approach and then to monotheism, and from monotheism finally to monism. In this way the transition of Indian religious pursuits in ancient India can be explained. The point is that man believed in the deification of Nature. In other words, from Nature to God or to a Supreme Power which is One was the passage of transition in man's spiritual outlook manifested in various religious practices.

It is said that such religious practices were not undertaken as without any desire or end in view which was mostly of an empirical nature. When man's spiritual vision enables him to concentrate on one Supreme Power, the end in view starts losing its empirical gains, and man is already in his path towards transcendental gain or his own spiritual realization, the expansion of his own self, crossing the boundaries of empiricality.

Similarly in music, there had been a tendency to associate some Deities with some specific *rasas*. But this tendency is more mythological than scientific. If it is taken too seriously then we should have to analyse music into two major component parts: (1) *rāga* and *rasa*, and (2) *rasa* and its *devatā*. The latter half constitutes the mythological part.

But a scientific treatment of music takes little time in getting rid of the latter half and tries to pay attention to the former. The episode of Nārada has a bearing on the latter half; but the scientific truth which it embodies is that a distorted performance of music will kill the basic *rasa* which predominates it. Not that any nymph or any Deity will be disfigured or mangled; but what will be killed is the *rasa* itself and with it the *rāgas* too; and to this we may add: music as such will be killed and along with it will also be killed the real, authentic man as the owner or the enjoyer of *rasa*.

There cannot be any music without a *rāga*; there cannot be any *rāga* without its indwelling *rasa*; there cannot be any *rasa* which does not infuse life to a *rāga*, and there cannot be any music which does not reveal a full-blooded growing life in the realization of a *rasa* through a *rāga*. This we accept. What we deny is: there cannot be any *rasa* without a presiding Deity. The assumptions of specific Deities corresponding to the *rasas* is rejected as being more mythological than logical.

Deifications of *rāgas* or *rāgas* having a definite motive empirically oriented are theories which have almost lost their credibility. The theory which is still accepted is that the *rāgas* are eloquent of *rasa*; the aesthetic appeal of a *rāga* as performed by a genuine musician with high dedication and consequent correct mastery of the technicalities are indubitably gaining more and more convincing and inspiring support by the present social culture, and in this sense can be said to have kept it alive and ever-growing.

So the main factor constitutive of the foundation of Indian music and musicology appears to be the close and intimate relation between a *rāga* (the sonal structure of melody) and its inherent *rasa*, and not between *rasa* and its so-called *devatā*. It is here that the science of acoustics can be and has been best suited to serve the cause of artistic enjoyment of eternal values. In other words, the main task of Indian musicology is to ensure the relation between acoustics and aesthetics. It should always be kept in mind that what is typically Indian in this context is the emphasis on the spiritual meaning of the situation regulating the universalization of eternal values as felt; the so-called conventional or primary or even secondary meanings belong to the empirical level and have no bearing on Indian musicology.

As said earlier that since a soul must inhabit a body, so a *rasa* is incarnated in a *rāga* which depends on a vocabulary of musical notes each signifying a particular *rasa*.

A pertinent question may be raised here: if every note is indicative of a particular *rasa* or if one note is indicative of more than one *rasa*, then are we to accept that a *rāga* consisting of seven notes would signify seven *rasas*, and a *rāga* consisting of six notes would signify six *rasas* and so on?

This is a very pertinent question indeed and before we try to formulate an answer to this question let us first try to see what are the *rasas* usually said to be associated with the *svaras*.

According to one theory, the notes *sā* and *ri* are both appropriate for the *rasas* of heroism, wonder and resentment; the note *dha* is suitable for the *rasas* of disgust and terror; the notes *gā* and *ni* are suitable for the *rasa* of grief or sorrow and the notes *ma* and *pa* are said to be appropriate for the *rasas* of humour and love respectively.

The distribution of *rasa* to *svara* as attributed to the spiritual vision of *Matanga* is as follows:

Sā and *Ri*	—	*Vira, Raudra* and *Adbhuta*
Gā	—	*Karuṇa*
Ma	—	*Hāsya*
Pa	—	*Śringāra*
Dha	—	*Vibhatsa, Bhayānaka*
Ni	—	*Karuṇa*

The characterisation of *svaras* according to their associated *rasas* as done by *Sārangadeva* is the same as above. The same is the case with *Bharata* in his *Nātyaśāstra*. The relevant *śloka* is:

Hāsyasṛngārayo kāryou Svarou Madhyamapancamou
Sādjṛshabhou tathā Caiba Viraroudrādbhuteṣu tu
Gāndhāraścha Nishādāscha kartyabyou Karuṇa Rase
Dhaibataścaiba Kartyabyo Vibhatse Sabhayānake.

It reads: *Hāsya* and *Śringāra rasas* are to be applied respectively through *ma* and *pa*; *Vira, Raudra* and *Adbhuta rasas* are to be manifested through the application of *sā* and *ri*; *Karuṇa rasa* to be revealed through *gā* and *ni*, and *Vibhatsa* and *Bhayānaka rasas* are to be expressed through *dha*.

Thus far there is no difficulty except that both *gā* and *ni* are meant to reveal the same *rasa*. But *Swāmi Prajnānānanda*[12] has referred to another view the source of which has not been clearly explained. According to such a view *Sā* is meant for *Vira, Ri* for *Raudra, Gā* for *Śānta, Ma* for *Hāsya, Pa* for *Śringāra, Dha* for *Vibhatsa* and *Ni* for

Karuṇa.

It will be seen that the difficulty regarding the double abode of *Karuṇa rasa* is overcome, but two of the *rasas* have been left out in the above scheme. What is unique is that it has made a provision for *Śānta rasa* which, though a debatable issue in the scheme of *rasa*, is important in so far as the tranquillity of mind or peace in the whole musical performance is considered essential in establishing an identity of the performer with his performance or of the outer man with the inner man. The importance of this *rasa* cannot be easily ignored in the domain of music.

Let us try to construct the following argument as a possible way out of this complicated picture.

The importance of *Śānta rasa* has not been recognised perhaps owing to the over-emphasis on Dramaturgy where there is little scope for the revelation of this *rasa*. But in other forms of artistic creation, where a large number of persons and a variety of situations are not involved, and a person is allowed to meditate with full concentration, he will be able, to achieve *Śānta rasa* or the peace of mind in its full calmness or tranquillity. Music may be regarded as some such situation where man can pursue the art alone quite far away from the doldrums of daily empirical life. The solitude which is a necessary precondition of spiritual realization will ensure the attainment of such an artistic enjoyment where the mind attains an ineffable pure joy within itself. Understood in this way, *Śānta rasa* is very much relevant in the context of Indian music and on the basis of such an analysis it may not be improper to interpret the *svara, ni* as indicative of *Śānta rasa*, whereas *gā* remains for *Karuṇa rasa*.

Another additional argument can be put forward which is more in keeping with the arrangement of notes in the standard scale. *Ni* being the last note may, with some propriety, be said to connote the peace of mind, or the *Śānta rasa* without disturbing *gā* which reveals *Karuṇa rasa*.

Thus we may, with some adequacy and desired faithfulness to the phenomenon of music as such, construct the following table showing the relation between the individual *svaras* and the associated *rasas* as their sole presiding factor in invoking specific artistic enjoyment:

Sā and *Ri*	— *Vira, Raudra* and *Adbhuta*
Gā	— *Karuṇa*
Ma	— *Hāsya*
Pa	— *Śringāra*
Dha	— *Vibhatsa* and *Bhayānaka*
Ni	— *Śānta*

To come back to the other important question raised earlier—whether a *rāga* consisting of several notes will have to be considered as expressing all the *rasas* as associated with the individual notes used. There is no weight in the question, since an apparent absurdity would be there as the obvious result.

But a closer examination will reveal that all the *rasas* are not equally embodied in a specific *rāga* even though several notes along with their associate *rasas* are used. The specific *rasa* which a *rāga* embodies is determined by the *rasa* of the dominant note or the *vādi svara*. In other words, it is the *vādi svara* which as the dominant note determines the specific character of the *rasa* which it indicates. The other auxiliary notes, *samvādi* or *vivādi*, act as helping instruments for a full and richer dimension of the *rasa* of the dominant note. Thus when a *rāga* is associated with a specific *rasa*, the inner significance is that the *rasa* of the *vādi svara* with the help of the *rasas* of other auxiliary *svaras* attempts to build up or invoke a general *rasa* expectedly in its full richness of appeal. The total *rasa* appeal of a *rāga* as performed may be correctly analysed into one fundamental *rasa* and other minor *rasas* supplementary to the fundamental *rasa*.

Again we fall back upon the analogy of human life as lived. If one takes care of the function of the heart, the functions of other organs are equally to be taken care of for the heart to function properly. Similarly, if we pay attention to lungs or stomach or kidney or liver, all other organs have to be equally looked after for a proper function of the whole system. Sometimes one organ plays the important role in being looked after and others act as auxiliary to it, and the picture might be changed when one of the previously auxiliary organs has to be looked after and the important one of the first case now plays the role of its auxiliary. This is clearly seen when a physician in trying to detect and cure a disease in a particular organ of a human being does successfuly cure the disease by distributing his attention to the relative importance of the role of other auxiliary organs and not only to that particular organ which is affected by the disease.

As a matter of fact music as such or even music as based on a specific melody is a *felt totality* where one *rasa* appears to be revealed as the main characterizing factor; but it is also enriched by the relative contribution of other *rasas* which in a given context play the role of minor *rasas* supplementary to the major one as indicated by the *vādi svara*. We are quite entitled to look at heart as the major organ of a living human body and others as supplementary; but at times we are also equally entitled to look at lungs or the stomach as the major one and in such cases heart would play the role of a minor organ. It all depends on how we look at the matter which is indeed a perfect totality where the relative contributions of human organs cannot be calculated with exact precision. Similar is the case with the *rāgas* which are perfect totalities as felt. All the *rasas* have their relative contributions. But to theoretically characterize the specific *rasa* of a *rāga*, one has to depend on the *rasa* appeal of the *vādi svara* as the chief guiding factor. The *vādi svaras* are differently indicated in different *rāgas* and this probably explains the necessary intermixture of *rasas* along with a dominant *rasa* in a melody-based musical performance. Music is not a mechanical combination of *svaras* or the *rasas*; the organisation of the note sequence in a *rāga* is done with the particular end in view that a totality of *rasa* appeal would emerge where there is a peaceful co-existence of all the other *rasas* as appropriate to the particular *svaras* used.

As another rough analogy, one can refer to the stage of *Henotheism* in early Vedic religion where according to the specific needs of human situation one among the multiplicity of Gods is taken to be the supreme, and prayers are made to appease Him, while others are regarded as subordinates. The picture changes in a change of situation where one among the so-called subordinates is taken to be the supreme God and others including the supreme God of the previous case becomes subordinate.

In music, there is nothing wrong here. On the contrary, it is intended by the aesthetic needs for a perfect creativity. Aesthetic pursuance of a single *rasa* in total isolation from all other *rasas* will result in a rather truncated form of artistic creation. For the fullness and growing richness in musical creativity all the *rasas* have to be taken together with a shared and balanced distribution of emphasis on other *rasas*, keeping in view one among them as fundamental according to the *intuitive verdict* of the creative artist. This requires a profound concentration and deep meditation on the part of the artist together with a perfect mastery over the technicalities in handling the musical notes—the vocabulary of *rasas*, in the plural.

The *rāgas* in Indian music are thus understood as *projecting* or constructing an abstract situation through an intermixture of several notes or several *rasas* associated with the notes with a balanced emphasis on a dominant *rasa* or its abode, the specific *vādi svara*. The *Vasanta rāga*, thus, is interpreted as the projection of joy of life suited to the spring season, *Megha rāga* to the advent of rains with all the exuberance of desire and opportunity for enjoyment. *Puravi* is considered as a typical evening *rāga* which is meant for the lamentation of Nature for the parting day. *Āśāvari* is the *rāga* connoting the melancholy pleading of a grievance for a just redress. *Bhairavi* is the finest example in Indian music depicting the *rasa* of love together with a devotional surrender to the highest principle of cosmic power. *Todi* is the surrender of the deer, the innocent creature in the animal kingdom to the magical and enchanting beauty of Nature. In this way, some abstract situations conducive to the specific *rasa* as embodied in the respective *vādi svaras* have been interpreted as *projections* of a successful musical creativity.

The *rāgamālā* paintings of Rajasthan are well-known for the pictorial presentation of the *projections* of the individual *rāgas*, where the underlying *rasa* has been clearly portrayed. But as regards the faithfulness or correctness of reproduction O.C. Gangoly[13] has made a very remarkable observation which is worth quoting here.

> It was at one time believed that the scheme of colours—in the distinct varieties of the colour-notes of the different parts of a rāgiṇi picture had a significant correspondence to the distinctive notes which made up the structure of the particular melody, the seven colours answering to the seven notes of the musical scale. The theory is very tempting, particularly with reference to the limited palettes of the early rāgiṇi 'primitives', but it is impossible to demonstrate that the artists of the rāgiṇi pictures were guided in their choice of particular colours used by any consideration of the structural, or sonal composition of the melodies they illustrated.

Whatever be the value or aesthetic importance of *rāgamālā* paintings, it has to be kept in mind that Indian music had never been thematic. The theme is a later construction belonging to a lower level, and it shows the relation between music and painting in a larger domain of artistic creativity. But so far as Indian music in its essentially pure form of self-realization is concerned it is wholly one of invoking the *rasa* or the mood in accordance with which the entire edifice of a *rāga* is created on the basis of the core-melodic pattern consisting of chosen notes and their proportionate, balanced sequence. The secret of revealing the associated *rasa* lies in the unique manner of treating the notes or any phrase of notes with an understood emphasis on the *vādi svara* together with relative emphasis on auxiliary *svaras*. No amount of pictorial representation or deification can do complete justice to the secret of the musical edifice thus created. This requires a pure and refined inner vision which the dedicated musician alone knows.

The ancient classification of *rāgas* into six major *rāgas* and thirty-six derived *rāgas*, six for each major one, or the classification of *rāgas* into masculine, feminine and neuter does not any longer hold ground. In the present days, all *rāgas* are treated alike. These are classified either by the *mela* system or by the *thāta* system. But neither of these systems can be claimed to be exhaustive because of the ever-growing immense dynamism of artistic creativity uncovering new horizons of *rāga* structures. The story that from the five faces of *Natarāja*, the cosmic dancer, came out five *rāgas* (*Sri, Vasanta, Bhairava, Pancama* and *Megha*) and that the sixth *rāga* (*Natanārāyana*) came out of the lips of *Pārvati* when she started her divine and elegant *lāsya* dance also is no longer acceptable as scientific.

In order to substantiate this point let us have a look at the classification of *rāgas* traditionally handed down to us by the ancient musicologists. The classification of these six archaic *rāgas* into thirty-six derived *rāgas* has been normally tabulated as follows:

1. Sri rāga (Melody of the Winter)

1.	2.	3.	4.	5.	6.
Goudi	*Kolāhali*	*Drāvali*	*Āndoliki*	*Mādhavi*	*Devagāndhāri*

2. Pancama rāga (Melody of the Autumn)

1.	2.	3.	4	5.	6.
Suddhanata	*Sāveri*	*Saindhavi*	*Mālati*	*Troti*	*Koumadaki*

3. Megha rāga (Melody of the Rainy Season)

1.	2.	3.	4.	5.	6.
Sourāstri	*Kāmbhāri*	*Vangāli*	*Madhumādhabi*	*Devakri*	*Bhupāli*

4. Natanārāyana (Melody of the Early Winter)

1.	2.	3.	4.	5.	6.
Vallabhā	*Mādhavi*	*Vidagdhā*	*Abhisārikā*	*Triveni*	*Megharanji*

The archaic *rāgas* of *Vasanta* and of *Bhairava*, are reportedly not available in the relevant text, *Sangeet Makaranda* by *Nārada*. *Bhairava* is accepted as the melody of the Summer and *Vasanta* as the melody of the Spring. We may record the full classification of six *rāgas* as available in *Rāga Darpana* in the following way:

1. Vasanta

1.	2.	3.	4.	5.	6.
Deśi	*Devagiri*	*Varāti*	*Todi*	*Lalitā*	*Hindoli*

2. Bhairav

1.	2.	3.	4.	5.	6.
Bhairavi	*Gurjari*	*Rāmakeli*	*Gunakeli*	*Saindhavi*	*Vangāli*

3. Sri rāga

1.	2.	3.	4.	5.	6.
Mālasri	*Triveṇi*	*Gouri*	*Kedāri*	*Madhumādhabi*	*Pahādi*

4. Pancama

1.	2.	3.	4.	5.	6.
Vibhāsa	*Bhupāli*	*Karnati*	*Vidāhamsika*	*Mālavi*	*Pātamanjari*

5. Megharāga

1.	2.	3.	4.	5.	6.
Mallāri	*Sourāthi*	*Sāveri*	*Kausiki*	*Gāndhāra*	*Harasringāra*

6. Natanārāyana

1.	2.	3.	4.	5.	6.
Kāmbodi	*Kalyāni*	*Ābhiri*	*Nātikā*	*Sārangi*	*Natta-Hāmir*

It is worth mentioning that *seasons* are not enough. One has to construct the specific *rasa* as appropriately conveying the mood and sentiment dominating a particular season and it is only in this way that a melody can be attributed to suitable seasons; otherwise not. And in this respect the traditional musicology is not sufficiently clear.

Again, *rāgas* have been classified to suit some particular hours of the cycle of the day. This is otherwise known as the *Time theory* of the *Rāgas*.

Under morning melodies are included *rāgas* like *Gāndhāra, Devagāndhāra, Saindavi, Nārāyani, Gurjari, Vangāla, Patamanjari, Vasanta, Malhāra, Lalit* and so on.

Under noon-day melodies are included *rāgas* like *Deśi, Kāmbhoji, Kaisiki, Madhumādhavi, Varāhaṃsa* and so on.

Under afternoon melodies are included *rāgas* like *Gauda* and its derivatives.

Under nocturnal melodies are included *rāgas* like *Suddhanata, Mālavagauda, Srirāga, Karnāta, Deśi* and so on.

This is in accordance with the classification as we find in *Sangeet-Makaranda*.

It will be clearly seen that there is an overlapping of *rāgas* in the above classification and what is more, this is in gross conflict with the classification of *rāgas* according to season. The simple and wisest approach seems not to attach too much importance to this type of attitude in classifying the melodies, because there is no uniform principle of classification. If *season* is more important, then *time* should not be allowed to interfere. The same could be said from the point of view of *time*. Moreover, there is wide divergence of opinion as regards the correct melody structure (or the specific *rāga* structure) of these *rāgas*, whether archaic or derived. Much controversy arises in determining the *vādi svara* even if, for arguments sake, some one fixed melody structure can be accepted regarding the respective *rāgas*. Most of the *rāgas* are obsolete and the *rāgas* which are still practised by the musicians are accepted within the framework of a particular *gharānā* interpretation making the situation too complicated to theorize systematically.

Musicology of the present day is being gradually stripped off its ancient mythological orientation. The arguments which are normally put forth for the division of *rāgas* into masculine, feminine etc., are that those *rāgas* are masculine which are the embodiments of the *rasa* of heroism and other presumably masculine attitudes. Similarly where the *rasa* of love, sorrow or humour is present, the resultant *rāgas* are treated as feminine because of the presumably feminine character of the *rasas* concerned. The *rasa* of terror, abhorrence or peace are considered to be neuter and the resultant *rāgas* are considered to be neuter melodies. One can easily detect the hollowness of such arbitrary analysis, since *rasa* as an artistic enjoyment at the transcendental level with a realized spiritual orientation ceases to have a definite character worth being characterized as masculine, feminine etc. As a matter of fact, all artistic enjoyments are neuter particularly at the transcendent level. The gender analysis of melodies is thus completely misleading. Moreover, the unique character of Indian music consists in creating a total *rasa* where several *rasas*, whether masculine or feminine, can be intertwined in such a subtle way that the alleged masculine or feminine character totally disappears. What shines forth is an abstract melody revealing an abstract feeling of a very high level of spiritual perfection in man's quest for self-realization within a tentatively cosmic perspective. The attitude of detachment from the mundane world is what is to be considered to be of utmost value and significance in the context of Indian music.

The freedom of the musician, which is universally accepted and which in Indian context lies in the supreme gift of improvisation, makes it possible for the musician to rise to the top of spiritual perfection in establishing a communion with the Infinite. No musicological theory or no performed music can claim to be final or complete. It can do so only at the cost of music itself. Indian music is thus an unending process, gradually unfolding itself in opening richer and richer domains of perfection, never final, never complete. It is perhaps the unique feature of Indian music wherein it differs from Western music and perhaps from all other forms of music in the world.

Music is an abstract art, and Indian music is perhaps the richest in such abstraction. Whatever descriptive imagery we come across in poems or in paintings falls far short of highest abstraction that Indian music tries to achieve through a balanced combination of musical sounds. The ultimate aim is to realize the noumenon behind the world of phenomena, to realize pure being as such within one's own being accompanied by pure bliss which spontaneously flows out of such realization. The ineffability of the creative projection on the basis of musical notes is always a self-transcending progress. The *creative* and the *ineffable* are the two catchwords of Indian music.

It may be argued that Indian music is emotionally decorative at the abstract level and is not illustrative. Its melodies have no concrete thematic scheme. It consists of the revelation of pure art values or abstract aesthetic enjoyments. There has been a tendency in modern painting to rise above the dictates of subject-matter in becoming essentially non-representative. But this tendency does not invalidate the ability of the painter to reproduce Nature or to translate human feelings and emotions into colours. The case of Indian music is, however, entirely different. The musician can be said to be basically incapable of reproducing anything concrete in Nature. One can indeed try to associate the appeal of Indian music with his own concrete feelings or situational emotions. But this is not what Indian music tries to achieve. If there is at all any emotion of love reflected by any Indian melody, it is to be interpreted as the "unsullied purity of love free from any desire" or if there is any feeling of sorrow, it is sorrow purified by renunciation. "Such are some of the radiant images which flit across the vision of Indian musical imagination", says O.C. Gangoly.[14] He concludes rightly that Indian music transcends our sense-experiences in any of its representation how much graceful or glorified they may be. It is a kind of music which transports us to a region of super-sensual ecstasy, an atmosphere of sublimity and spiritual enjoyment.

It should be kept in mind that such an analysis of Indian music applies quite properly to music which is lyric-free and not to music which is lyric-dependent. The former and not the latter may be said to constitute the essence of Indian music.

NOTES AND REFERENCES

1. In this chapter I have tried to construct the views of Rabindranath on Indian music and musicology on the basis of his remarks, lectures, dialogues and discussions on music as incorporated in his *Sangeet Chinta*.
2. Similar other cases can be considered as worth mentioning. We need not dwell at length on this point because this may be out of context here.
3. W. Kandinsky—The Doctrine of Internal Necessity, as incorporated in *Creativity in the Arts* edited by V. Tomas.
4. For a detailed treatment of the concept and evolution of *Rāga* see Swami Prajnanananda—*A History of Indian Music*.
5. The Concept of Rasa as incorporated in *Studies in Philosophy* edited by Prof. Gopinath Bhattacharya.
6. *Ibid*., p. 350.
7. *Ibid*., p. 351.
8. *Ibid*., p. 355.
9. To this point we have already made a passing reference in the chapter on 'Music and Man'.
10. *Studies in Philosophy*, p. 357. For a detailed analysis see K.C. Bhattacharya's paper on 'The Concept of Rasa'. Only the major points of his profound treatment have been reproduced here for the sake of relevance to the present discussion.
11. O.C. Gangoly—*Rāgas & Rāginis*, p. 99.
12. *Rāga-O-Rupa*, p. 119.
13. *Rāgas & Rāginis*, pp. 101 (F.N.)-102.
14. *Ibid*., p. 161.

CHAPTER 8

RABINDRANATH TAGORE ON INDIAN MUSICOLOGY
A Critical Appraisal

In our task of constructing the views of Rabindranath on Indian music and musicology, we now propose to enter into a detailed and systematic account of his experiments which are more polemic than expository.

The main thrust of his reactions may be summed up in the following observations:

(a) There is not and cannot be any blue-print of Indian music.

(b) *Rāgas* are to be interpreted entirely according to the mood reflected by the totality of performance and not according to what is a *vādi svara* in a given melody. Musicological injunctions should not always be rigidly followed.

(c) Lyric-free music and instrumental music in particular are the purest forms of Indian music constituting perhaps the very essence of Indian music.

(d) Improvisation which is the unique characteristic feature of Indian music should not be extended too far since there is the danger of distorting the intended appeal of a given melody. The freedom of the musician should be strictly in accordance with the spirit of music.

(e) Western music is mainly dominated by harmony; but Indian music is mainly dominated by melody; and as such, unlike the Western musician, the Indian musician is at once the composer and the performer.

(f) The transcendental or the eternal value (*as felt*) which constitutes the artistic enjoyment in Indian music is the cosmic essence or the *Viśva rasa*.

(g) *Deśi* songs may be composed in a more sophisticated manner following the mould of the traditionally accepted melody-patterns.

(h) Indian music overflows national boundaries.

Rabindranath Tagore, the greatest musicologist of the present times, has composed nearly two thousand songs. He is the poet, the painter and the musician,—the three in one; and for this reason he has visualised Indian music from a completely non-traditional and non-conventional point of view. Rabindranath, the musicologist, can be best understood through his songs—the lyric and the melody—both his own composition. He elevated his poems into songs; but he never translated his songs into paintings. From this, one is prompted to conclude that the poet did not believe in the pictorial representation of music. To this point we have already made some remarks in connection with our brief discussion on *Rāgamālā* paintings in the preceding chapter. The songs of Rabindranath always have an appeal to the universal spirit of man. We shall try to analyse and construct his views on musicology without analysing the greatness of his poetry but with the help of his own composition of melodies.

In some of his *Brahma-sangeet* and other songs he has closely followed the *Dhrupad* style in its purity and sanctity free from all the ornamental decorations. The *tālas* chosen are sometimes *Dhāmār* or *Choutāl* or *Surfāktāl*. He is not much in favour of the *Kheyāl* style of singing, because he thinks it to be more of exhibitionism of the musicians' skill of performance than of the spiritual essence of pure classical music. His *bāul, keertan* and *tappā* style of songs are said to be influenced by the indigenous folk-music of Bengal; he does not follow the quick and oscillating *tāns* which are to be found in the *tappā* of *Shorimiān*. He has composed some songs which are based on traditional *Kheyāl*; but he has abandoned the *tān aṅga*.

Some of the *rāgas* of traditional Indian music which Rabindranath has utilised in composing his own melody structure are broadly the following:

(a) *Yaman Kalyān* — *Sundara Bahe Ānanda*
(b) *Puravi* — *Asru Nadeer Sudoor pade*
(c) *Bhairav* — *Mana Jago Mangalaloke*
(d) *Khāmāj* — *Tomāri Gehe Pālichho*
(e) *Āsāvari* — *Tomār Sur Śunāye*
(f) *Gurjari Todi* — *Prabhāte Vimala Ānande*
(g) *Nata Malhār* — *More Bāre Bāre*
(h) *Darbāri Kānāda* — *Ebār Nirab Kore Dāo He*
(i) *Behāg* — *Mahārāj Eki Sāje*
(j) *Mālkaus* — *Ānandadhārā Bahichhe Bhubane*
(k) *Bāgeśri* — *Ye Rāte Mor Duyār Guli*
(l) *Bāhar* — *Āji Kamala Mukula dala*
(m) *Adānā* — *Mandire Mama Ke Āshile*

(n) *Bhairavi* — *Ayi Ye Tari Dilo Khule*
(o) *Chhāyānat* — *He Sakhā, Mamo Hridaye Raho*
(p) *Deshmalhār* — *Esho Śyamala Sundara,*

and there are similar others also. But it should be mentioned that there is hardly any well-known and popular *rāga* which did not receive its due importance in the hands of the poet. Some of the so-called South Indian *rāgas* have also their role in the poet's melodic compositions, *Latāngi* and *Singhendra-madhyam*, for example, to mention a few.* As regards new experiments of traditional *rāga* structures, the name of *Kāzi Nazrul Islām* also deserves mention. But we do not propose to discuss the dimensions of his creative music in this context. Rabindranath has a definite musicological point of view, and it is exclusively for this reason that we have taken up the music of Tagore for our present study.

If we analyse the historical evolution of *rāga* structures, we shall come across a constant change of emphasis in the classification of *rāgas* and in selecting the major *rāgas* and their derivatives. The following synoptic list may be of some help in understanding the change of emphasis.

According to *Dattila* (second century A.D.) the *rāgas* were located as independent and autonomous *Jātis*. The names one may find in his work are *Sādjā-Kaisiki, Rakta-gāndhāri, Āndhri, Nandayanti* and so on. *Bharata* (third century A.D.) mentions eighteen *Jātis* of which seven are said to belong to *Sādjā-grāma* and the rest to *Madhyama-grāma*. *Gāndhāra-grāma* seems to be obsolete as belonging to the kingdom of Gods. Between approximately fifth and seventh century *Matanga* speaks of *Rāga-gitis, Sādhārana-gitis, Bhāsā-gitis* and *Vibhāsā-gitis*. One finds here the mention of *Takka-rāga, Souviraka, Pancama, Bhinna-sādjā, Mālava-Kaisika, Votta-rāga, Hindolaka, Takka-Kaisika*. It is perhaps at this stage that the vision of the ancient musicologists started being articulated into some apparently systematic structures which were subsequently formulated as *rāgas* with a definite melodic pattern. But unfortunately the so-called definite pattern was merely tentative and underwent drastic transformations in the characterization of the definite notes in the body of the basic patterns themselves. The classification made by *Nārada* (between seventh and ninth century) we have already mentioned in the preceding chapter.

It was about eleventh century that we come across a classification in the full from six major *rāgas* (*Janaka*) into thirty-six derived *rāgas*

**Bāaje Karuna Sure* is in *Singhendra-madhyam* and *Hridaye Tomār Dayā Yeno Pāi* is in *Latāngi*.

(*Janya*) done by *Mammata*, author of *Sangeet-ratna-mālā*. The six *rāgas* are: *Karnāta, Nata, Megha, Desākh, Mālava* and *Vasanta*. These are all supposed to be *suddha rāgas*. The classification of *rāgas* into *suddha, salāga* and *samkirṇa* was first done by *Locana* in about 1000 A.D. Then the classification went on in diverse directions.[1] One may perhaps reasonably cut short the detailed analysis by mentioning a few important ones in the following table:

1.	*Brahmā* (Date cannot be traced)	*Sri, Vasanta, Bhairav, Pancama, Megh* and *Nata.*
2.	*Sangeet Ratnākara (Sārangadeva*: 1210-1247 A.D.)	*Vasanta, Vrihannata, Malhār, Mālava, Kaisika* and *Pradip.*
3.	*Sangeet-Samaya-sāra (Pārśadeva*: 1250 A.D.)	*Bhairav, Bhupāla, Śri, Patmanjari, Vasanta, Mālava* and *Vangāla.*
4.	*Rāgārnava* (Author not known to us: 1300 A.D.)	*Bhairav, Pancama, Nata, Malhāra, Gouda-mālava* and *Desākh.*
5.	*Pancama Samhitā (Nārada*: 1440 A.D.)	*Mālava, Malhāra, Śri, Vasanta, Hindola* and *Karnāta.*
6.	*Rāga-Darpaṇa (Dāmodar Misra*: 1625 A.D.)	*Sri, Vasanta, Bhairav, Pancama, Megh* and *Nata-nārāyana.*
7.	*Anupa-Sangitāngkusa (Bhāva-Bhatta*: 1674 A.D.)	*Bhairav, Mālava-Kousika, Hindola, Dipaka, Sri* and *Megha.*

We need not lengthen the list. One thing is clear that some new *rāgas* are coming into being, while some others are being dropped. Moreover, some *rāgas* have a steady appeal in different stages of historical development, for example, *Sri, Bhairav, Vasanta, Mālava, Pancama* and similar others. From this one is tempted to draw the conclusion that the spiritual vision of musicologists has always been alive and new experiments have always been there. It is not until we come across the monumental work done by *Pandit Bhātkhande*[2] that we find a very systematic account of a list of *Thāta rāgas*, the major melody scale or the parent *rāgas* with a definite note sequence in the ascending order. The table may be constructed as follows:

1.	*Bilāwal*	— S R G M P D N—all *suddha svaras*
2.	*Bhairavi*	— S R G M P D N—R G D N—*Komala*
3.	*Bhairav*	— S R G M P D N—RD—*Komala*
4.	*Āsāvari*	— S R G M P D N—G D N—*Komala*
5.	*Todi*	— S R G Ḿ P D N—RGD—*Komala*, M—*Teevra*
6.	*Kalyān*	— S R G Ḿ P D N—M—*Teevra*
7.	*Kāfi*	— S R G M P D N—GN—*Komala*
8.	*Puravi*	— S R G Ḿ P F N—RD—*Komala*, M—*Teevra*
9.	*Mārwā*	— S R G Ḿ P D N—R—*Komala*, M— *Teevra*
10.	*Khāmāj*	— S R G M P D N—N—*Komala*

There are several derivative *rāgas*, a large variety indeed, which are grouped under one or other of these ten *thātas* (*rāgas*). These *thātas* are not called *rāgas* in the strict sense, because they indicate only the ascending order of the notes concerned. A *rāga* requires, in addition, a descending order and also the dominant notes together with a definite rule of treatment (*pakad*). But corresponding to the names of the *thāta*, there are some *rāgas* having the same name. So, with some reservation, the *thātas* are called *rāgas* keeping in view only those bearing the same name.

Though the list is not accepted as comprehensive and some overlapping features are discernible in the derivative *rāgas*, this table is, even today, accepted as the most effective guideline in the classification of *rāgas*, particularly in *Hindustāni* music.

Whether in the ancient period or in the modern period, it will be noticed that no uniform principle of classification has been followed. As regards the ancient classification one is at a loss to decipher what was the exact note sequence of a *rāga* chosen under the classified table.

In view of this controversial aspect regarding the exact character of the note sequence of a *rāga* in the ancient period and further in view of the unavailability of the principle of classification,[3] one is prompted to say that Indian musicology cannot provide any blue-print.[4] The musicologists have full freedom in creating the melodies which in their opinion suited best their own spiritual vision. No damage indeed has been done to Indian music; on the contrary, it helps the music to grow from its infancy to childhood and from childhood to a full-grown man.

There is yet another sense in which it can be said that Indian music cannot be reduced to any blue-print. The immense ornamentation by which a *rāga* is rendered by the musicians from their own intuitive realization of the basic appeal of the *rāga* cannot be tabulated in a fixed notation system. Moreover, *meends* and *gamakas* which add to the aesthetic embellishment of Indian music cannot be demonstrated in any notational picture. The particular *srutis* used in some special *rāgas* (*Śri* and *Darbāri Kānāda* for example) are beyond any mathematical calculation to be properly drawn on papers with exact accuracy. This constitutes one of the several unparallel (unique) features of Indian music which is to be left entirely to the musician's spiritual realization. This is one of the several reasons why in Indian music the composer and the performer are and should be the same. The greatest musicians of the West are greatest composers. But the picture is different in Indian music. The greatest musicians of India are greatest composers and also performers at the same time. As a matter of fact, composition proceeds along with performance.

From this, Rabindranath takes the issue and is emboldened to make his fresh experiments with Indian music. His revolutionary outlook should not be interpreted as the total renunciation of the antiquity; rather it is a revolution with a shift of emphasis and a change in outlook. About Rabindranath it is said: Perhaps no living poet was more religious and no man of religion was more poetical than this great Indian. We can safely formulate this by saying: Perhaps no living musician was more spiritual and no man of spiritualism was more musical than this great Indian. Rabindranath has created his melodies in his search for the true wealth and power of the inner spirit which is always vibrating to find a suitable medium of reflecting and manifesting itself; and Music is the result through which he is face to face with the deepest and innermost in him. Indian music has always been *catholic* in the sense of assimilating new experiments and at the same time *puritan* in the sense of rigidity of practice as regards what should be followed in music once it is ensured by meditation and intuitive realization. It is liberal in the sense that the most important thing is the musician's own ability to be delighted in his music; it is, again, conservative in the sense that the musician's freedom in creativity is not the interplay of his whimsical ideas.

With this granted liberalism in Indian music along with the prescribed conservative boundaries Rabindranath proceeds to argue that *rāgas* should be classified not arbitrarily, nor according to the *vādi-samvādi* notes, but purely according to the *rasas* which the *rāgas* are expected to invoke. Presumably he is not happy with the *Bhātkhande* system of classification, not merely for the reason that it is not comprehensive, but also for the reason that perhaps it is misleading. *Mālkaus* would be a good example to establish this point. It is said to belong to *Bhairavi Thāta*; but the *rasa* it reflects is far from that which is reflected in *Bhairavi*. Moreover, *Bhairavi* is customarily treated as a morning *rāga*, but *Mālkaus* is said to belong to midnight, where apart from all things, freshness could not be said to be present. (Again, the *vādi svara* in *Mālkaus* is *ma* which admittedly reflects the *rasa* of *Hāsya*; but the total aesthetic appeal of this *rāga* is obviously far from this specific *rasa*. Similarly *Yaman Kalyān* does not reveal the *rasa* of *Karuṇa* even though *Gā* is accepted to be *vādi* here.) The popular *rāga*, *Komala rishava Āsāvari*, would not come under *Āsāvari Thāta* because of the use of *Komala rishava*. Many similar other inconsistencies may be pointed out, and we need not multiply instances. Enough it is to say that *rāgas*, traditionally accepted as pure *rāgas*, like *Behāg*, *Kedār*, *Lalit*, *Bāhār*, *Desh* and many others where two notes of the chromatic scale, a note and its sharp or flat (like two *madhyamas* or two *nishādas*), are both used will fall outside the *thātas* as codified by *Pandit Bhātkhande*. The *thātas* are perhaps not meant for interpreting any *rāga*. But how could he explain the grouping of several *rāgas* under a *thāta*?

Rabindranath is of opinion that *rāgas* are to be interpreted or classified according to the mood or sentiment they reflect. Since music is the spontaneous flow of the inner spiritual vision of man (does not matter to what extent it undergoes ornamentations through long cultivation of *svara sādhanā* or practice on musical scales) a *rāga* is always the musical medium through which man expresses his innermost feelings, his joy, his sorrow, his anger, his wonder, and last but not the least, his peace of mind. He appeals to the musicologists to look through the specific notes which may be regarded as most appropriate in conveying such inner feelings in man. Instead of spending time and energy in establishing what should be the *vādi* or the *samvādi svara* in specific *rāgas* like *Multāni* or *Kedār* or *Yaman Kalyān*, we should be careful to discover what should be the *vādi-samvādi svara* for a *rāga* of joy, a *rāga* of sorrow and so on. The specific notes and their proportionate sequence in ascending and descending order were already finalised long ago. There is no use in debating on this point any more. On the contrary what is needed most and has not been done yet is the thorough classification of *rāgas* strictly according to the specific *rasas* of which the *rāgas* are the so-called living embodiments. It is through the *rāgas* that the inherent *rasas* are fully articulated. Rabindranath goes far ahead in suggesting that we might forego the attempts in naming the *rāgas* which are meaningless symbols and instead we might name the *rāgas* in conformity with the basic *rasas* as unfolded. The *rāgas* depicting the feeling of sorrow should have a slow tempo as the painful night appears to be of a much longer duration with its slow movement of pace; the *rāgas* depicting the feeling of joy should, on the other hand, have a quick tempo since the joyous moments of life appear to be very short-lived. In such *rāgas* the use of galloping notes might be of richer effect. In other words, the main point of argument which Rabindranath wants to put forward is that in classifying or interpreting a *rāga* the emotional essence or the *rasa* should be the major determinant factor; the melodic details and the rhythmic pattern may be ascertained later on which are not as important as the main essence of the *rāga* itself.

What is of utmost importance in music, according to Rabindranath, is the discovery of the melodies which will convey 'the supreme faith of love, the faith of life in death, of the victory in defeat, of the power hidden in the frailness of beauty, of the dignity of pain that accepts hurt, but disdains to return it.' This is the true transcendental spirit looming behind the aesthetic appeal of Indian music. This is how the *rasas* gain the needed transcendental interpretation in the hands of Rabindranath.

On the basis of the same *rāga* several melodies may be composed which might be all different in their musical ornamentations or in their technique of presentation, the mode of characterizing. But again, several melodies of the same *rāga* are the same in so far as they reflect the same ethos. But the *rāga* in its essential structure is fixed. It is more fixed than the mode and less fixed than the melody. Beyond the mode and beneath the melody, the *rāga* stands as a perfect nucleus richer in significance than a given mode or a given melody. It is this nucleus which is of fundamental importance and has to be interpreted not only with care but with motherly affection in discovering the *rasa* which is the key to its proper understanding. Whether it is the joy of union, or inspiration of joy or the stress of pain or the storm of passion, or the pang of separation or the thrill of expectation, each *rāga* stands for the inner view of the soul and one has to work this deeper meaning in classifying or codifying the *rāgas*. All the so-called principles, whether one or many, are rather arbitrarily imposed by the musicologists of antiquity or of the modern times and they appear to forget that the *rāgas* are intrinsically human, carrying the message of the human soul. This is the typical or unique character of Indian *mārga sangeet*. Rabindranath refers to a very revealing analogy. He says that the best part of music is lost when the appropriate melody is missing; thereby its movement and colour are lost and it becomes like a butterfly whose wings have been plucked.[5]

We would be failing in our duty if we refrain from referring to a Western contrary and a parallel on this issue. This is by Schopenhauer.[6] He argues:

> The composition of melody, the disclosure in it of all the deepest secrets of human willing and feeling, is the work of genius, whose action, which is more apparent here than anywhere else, lies far from all reflection and conscious intention, and may be called an inspiration. The conception is here, as everywhere in art, unfruitful. The composer reveals the inner nature of the world, and expresses the deepest wisdom in a language which his reason does not understand; as a person under the influence of mesmerism tells things of which he has no conception when he awakes. Therefore, in the composer, more than in other artist, the man is entirely separated and distinct from the artist.

This is the Western contrary. In Indian music the performer and the composer are the same person. The artist in performing music spontaneously composes by immensely proportionate measures of improvisation, an idea which is entirely alien to Western music. The Indian performer as an artist is never separated from the composer. Sometimes the performer in the act of his performance composes many intricate patterns of note combinations which he neither thought before, nor could remember afterwards. As regards the parallel, the observation of Schopenhauer runs:

> As quick transition from wish to satisfaction and from satisfaction to a new wish, is happiness and well-being, so quick melodies without great deviations are cheerful; slow melodies, striking painful discords, and only winding back through many bars to the key-note are, as analogous to the delayed and hardly won satisfaction, sad. The delay of the new excitement of will, languor, could have no other expression than the sustained keynote, the effect of which would soon be unbearable; very monotonous and unmeaning melodies approach this effect.

One can readily see the similarity of interpretation when Rabindranath speaks of slow melodies as those of sorrow and quick melodies as those of joy. He has pointed out that music becomes monotonous and distortive if too much artificial emphasis is given on a sustained note with undue stress not warranted by the aesthetic needs. He draws our attention to the aspect of proportion and restraint in being faithful to the demands of art in music.

Indian music is mostly *solo* oriented; whereas Western music is mainly *orchestra* (symphony) oriented. This is how Rabindranath would view the difference in approach in the two kinds of music. According to the needs of orchestration, due emphasis must have to be given to *harmony*:

on the other hand, emphasis is always on *melody* in Indian music to reveal the individual's own attitude which is his own treasure of realization.

According to Rabindranath, melody and harmony are like lines and colours in painting. A simple linear picture may be completely beautiful. But the introduction of colour may make it vague and prosaic. Yet, colour may, by combination of lines, create great paintings as long as it does not destroy the intrinsic value. Rabindranath with his characteristic liberal approach and open-mindedness would argue that harmony in Indian music should not be condemned only because it is the Western style of music presentation. If harmony were the artificial product of a particular foreign culture based on superstition, then of course its claim could have been set aside. But to ignore it altogether only because it belongs to a foreign culture would be too much. The case appears to be as if a surgery could not be applied to the body of an Indian patient only because it is being invented and practised by foreign doctors. If it is necessary to cure a disease and if no exact Indian substitute is available, it is wiser to adopt that course of action for the longer interest of the life of the patient. Similarly, if it can be accommodated in Indian music to meet aesthetic demands, then there is possibly no harm. Harmony in music is something real and genuine. And we would be unwisely obstinate if it is denied that the incompleteness in perfection of Indian music is owing to the absence of harmony.

But it may be pointed out in reply that the absence of harmony does not undermine the magnanimity of Indian music; on the contrary, its introduction might cause enough harm in damaging the supreme melodic excellence of Indian *rāga* music. A master musician can indeed assimilate harmony in Indian music, if and only if the fundamental melodic appeal remains undisturbed, and is in need of being enriched by the introduction of harmony as a compensatory value.

To come back to our original issue with which we started.

The general tendency of European music is to reveal the rhythm of the eternal flow of diversity of events and phenomena of the empirical world. The general tendency of Indian music is to withdraw from all empirical diversifications in search for the underlying unity which can be reached only through meditation, the deep, the secret, the only one which stands calm and quiet in its serenity in the background of the vastness of the sky. European music, says Rabindranath, reminds us of the surface waves of the ocean, their ever-changing rhythm and colourful breaks in a huge multiplicity of sparkling flashes; Indian music, on the other hand, reminds us of the unfathomable depth of the ocean where it is dumb and mum, far beneath the multiplicity of waves on the body of its surface. Indian music is thus the music for the *One*; but the one is not the *lonely one*; it is the one which is the *universal one*, the same everywhere in the Universe and not the one in the dark, lonely corner of the world.

Rabindranath, in view of his observations above, concludes that the *rasa* of Indian music is the *viśva-rasa*; it is the cosmic essence, the cosmic ethos. The rain reflected in the *rāga Megh* is not the rain in front of my house; it is the rain of the Universe. The sorrow is not my sorrow as it is of today; it the sorrow of mankind of the world. The idea of cosmic ethos is a necessary addendum to the transcendental character of the artistic enjoyment or *rasa*. The former follows from the latter.

Rabindranath has taken particular care in being faithful to all the nine *rasas* as admitted by the ancient musicologists. In *Sangeet Dāmodara* by *Subhankara*, the *sloka* about nine *rasas* runs as follows:

> *Sringārahāsyakaruṇā Raudrabirabhyānakah*
> *Vibhatsādbhutaśāntaśca Nava Nātyarasāh Smritāh.*

The meaning is too clear to elaborate. A reference may be made to the following songs of Rabindranath depicting each of the above nine *rasas*:[7]

(1) *Māyābanabihārini Harini—Śringāra*
(2) *Amrā nā gān gāyoār dal re—Hāsya*
(3) *Sundarer Bandhan Nisthurer—Karuṇa*
(4) *Jageni Ekhono Jage ni—Raudra*
(5) *Āspardhā Eki Toder—Vira*
(6) *Nām Laho Devatār—Bhayānaka*
(7) *Arjun, Tumi Arjun—Adbhuta*
(8) *O mā, O mā, Phiriye ne—Vibhatsa*
(9) *Hridayanandana Bone—Śānta.*

The greatest disadvantage in heaven, in the kingdom of Gods, is that everything is perfect, everything is complete. There is nothing for the Gods to do or to create; the Gods suffer from a sort of divine indolence. The greatest advantage of this world is its imperfection or incompleteness which prompts man to go ahead in making it perfect and complete and it is in this pursuit that music as a creative art has come into being in the eternal quest of man towards self-perfection. Music of this world, as conceived by Rabindranath, is worth pursuing because it is incomplete, because we have not yet attended the perfection we are driving at. Nobody knows how far and how long we have to go. The innumerable *rāgas* are inexhaustible attempts of mankind to comprehend the essence or *rasa* of the universe in small or large vessels of *rāgas* according to our limited capacity of the inner resources. But our principal aim is to make the vessels larger and larger, to make them more and more comprehensive, to embrace the whole universe into our bosom.

The transcendental character of *rasa* or the *viśva-rasa* has also been acknowledged by Schopenhauer,[8] and here he comes very near to the spirit of Indian music. He argues that music never expresses "the phenomena, but only the inner nature, the in-itself of all phenomena, the will itself. It does not, therefore, express this or that particular or definite joy, this or that sorrow, or pain or horror or delight, or merriment or peace of mind; but joy, sorrow, pain, horror, delight, merriment, peace of mind themselves, to a certain extent in the abstract, their essential nature, without accessories, and therefore without their motives. Yet we completely understand them in this extracted quintessence." The striking similarity of approach with Rabindranath is too obvious to be worked out in details.

In pursuing his so-called revolutionary approach Rabindranath strongly argues that the *rāgas* or the basic melody-patterns should not overpower the *rasa,* but that the contrary should always be the case. The main objective of a particular melody and of music as such is to convey the innermost feelings of man; and according to the specific dimensions of such feelings music has been given the specific shape in the form of specific melodies. He holds that the human feelings have been, as it were, handed over to the respective melody-patterns to be taken care of properly; but instead, the painful result is that, as if, by an act of treachery the melodies have killed the feelings and have become the supreme lord, nothing to take care of or look after. Rabindranath laments that one is now interested to see whether the theoretical structure of *Jay-Jayanti* or *Kānāda* or *Behāg* is being faithfully maintained; there is no concern for whether the respective feelings working in the background of the *Rāgas* are being properly reflected. This should not be the case and the entire picture has to be reversed, the other way round. He goes ahead to hold that we are not blindly obliged to the theory of the *rāgas*; rather we are obliged to the fundamental human feelings behind the *rāgas* and for its faithful revelation minor changes in the theoretical structure, if necessary, should be unhesitantly incorporated by the musician himself. In his own words: if the emphasis on *pancama* instead of *madhyama* is more conducive to the expression of the specific feeling intended by a *rāga* (he mentions of *Jay-Jayanti*) then that has to be followed, no matter if it results in the destruction of the so-called *rāga* itself. We are not bribed by the *rāgas*, he argues, so that we have to maintain its structure at any cost. Such attitude of blind slavery to the theory of the *rāgas* should be totally abandoned.

This is an extreme attitude, indeed. Perhaps Rabindranath has in view some cases, which he might have come across in his experience, where the musicians, having not attained the requisite mastery over the technicalities of the *rāgas*, pursued their performance in rendering the *rāgas* with no adequate vision or the depth of feeling.

Not that such cases do never occur. But our appeal to Rabindranath is not to take such cases seriously. The deviation of notes, if done, has to be done with great caution so that the main emphasis within the structure of a particular *rāga* is not disturbed and at the same time proper justice is done to the feeling in the background. If we make major changes in the theoretical structure of a *rāga* and try to defend it in the name of our feeling, then of everything else the *rāga* would not be as it should be; it would be the rendering of a completely different *rāga*. Minor changes are always permissible and perhaps it is for this reason that the ancient musicologists took great pains in determining the *vādi, samvādi, vivādi* and *anuvādi svaras*. If the requisite feeling is not there, the fault is not with the theoretical structure of the *rāga*, but with the musician who has distorted it by failing to manipulate the major guiding notes specified in the *rāga* structure. He is the ideal musician of India who renders the *rāga* so faithfully with his perfect mastery that the impression should be, as it were, that some intrinsic feeling is trying to speak itself out through some notes, no matter which *rāga* it is which these notes belong to, or no matter whether we understand it or identify it to be a particular *rāga*.

The whole matter in the hands of Rabindranath appears to be as if we should be prepared to kill the body at the cost of the soul. Music being a performing art, the aspect of rendering the *rāga-rupa* is of utmost importance; there is no doubt about that. But such performance should have a theoretical guideline at some stages, perhaps at the initial stage, only to act as the helping factor and not as the sole determining factor in the musician's expression of feeling. We agree that musicological injunctions should not be blindly followed. But it is one thing to follow the injunctions blindly and another, to follow them with proper realization. The former is not, but the latter is, what is intended by Indian musicology. Moreover, the so-called musicological theories should not be taken as injunctions externally imposed upon the musicians. They may be regarded as injunctions of the musician's soul, the injunctions of his inner realization. This is what the law of intrinsic necessity in Indian musicology tries to focus. To take a more concrete illustration of this issue.

In composing the melody of a song Rabindranath himself has chosen the *rāga Bāgeśri*; but instead of following the standard theoretical formulation he makes a change in *nishāda*; he uses *suddha nishāda* instead of *komala nishāda* as prescribed in the theory. Rabindranath himself has used two *dhaivatas* and two *nishādas*, the *suddha* and the *komala*, in his rendering of *rāga Bhimpalaśree*; the use of two *dhaivatas* may be found in the case with *Puravi*. In his treatment of *Āsāvari* we find the application of both the *rishavas*; again, he has avoided sharp (*teevra*) *madhyama* in his rendering of the *rāga Rāmkeli*. In some cases, he has used *Behāg* with two *nishādas* and so on.[9] What would be our reaction? It is three-fold:

(a) One can say that Rabindranath has distorted the *Rāga*: he is unaware of the theoretical structure;

(b) One can say that Rabindranath is quite aware, but *suddha nishāda* would be more helpful in conveying his own feeling which he intends to convey in conformity with the lyric;

(c) One can say that it is not *Rāga Bāgeśri* but something else.

Of the three reactions, the first one is the weakest and rejected straightaway. The third one is the strongest and there is no harm in giving it a separate name; even though Rabindranath himself has not chosen a different name for this melody. The second alternative is rather puzzling which can, however, be settled by pointing out that minor changes in the notes are quite permissible within the framework of Indian musicology. And master musicians do frequently introduce minor changes without affecting the total appeal of the *rāga* and this, on the contrary, elevates the aesthetic embellishment in the employment of the *rāga*. The resultant *rāga* would be called by the same name and it is quite an acceptable fact that the same *rāga* has different dimensions of appeal in the hands of different musicians; the secret lies in the mastery of handling the notes and the depth of inner vision.

Rabindranath perhaps has been scared with his rather unfortunate experience of some untrained (or not properly trained) musicians who wanted to exhibit the skill of their performance and in this way destroyed the inner feeling of the *rāga*; with their limited abilities they tried to maintain the theoretical structure of the *rāga* and as a result the emphasis has been misplaced to the total neglect of the *rasa* appeal of the *rāga* concerned. Indeed, one is at perfect liberty to create new *rāgas* according to one's own realization and in this sense one can have a new interpretation of any *rāga* which is not foreseen by the traditional musicologists. The great merit of Indian musicology lies in its liberal attitude to make room for new innovations towards richer and newer creativity. This we have already mentioned. Rabindranath is right in his view that the names of the *Rāgas* are not important. In fact, names are used only to act as some artificial identification marks. Our main concern is not that what *rāga* is being performed, or what *rāga* according to what interpretation at what period of history is being performed; it is always that what music is being rendered and with what aesthetic appeal in the background.

Similarly in his revolutionary attitude in denouncing the importance of *Sam* in the *tāla* system, Rabindranath has said that to come back to *Sam* in the course of performance *at any cost* is not a proper aesthetic attitude. As a result, he is in favour of eliminating the importance of *Sam*. But it will be seen, our appeal again to Rabindranath, that coming back to *Sam* must always be spontaneous and it is never to be done at the cost of anything, still less *at any cost*. The performer with his perfect aesthetic vision and with perfect mastery over his own abilities always points out the *Sam* smoothly and spontaneously creating the effect that the emphasis on *Sam* is really needed here by aesthetic consideration. Rabindranath, perhaps, is under the influence of the Western system of free rhythm, and he is perfectly at liberty to compose new *tāla* patterns with no *sam* in them. But he would be wrong, if his critical views are influenced by sub-standard musical performance by untrained or under-trained musicians, by musicians lacking the requisite aesthetic vision.

Now we come to the most important part of the musical creativity of Rabindranath with reference to the distinction between lyric-free and lyric-dependent Indian music, and the role of improvisation, the unique feature of Indian music.

In his songs Rabindranath seems to have reached the height of his aesthetic excellence and his own spiritual vision. He composed the lyric and he composed the melody according to the feelings conveyed by his lyric.

Though his superb creativity is revealed through his songs (music as lyric-based or music as wedded to words), Rabindranath boldly declares that lyric-free music, or the instrumental music in particular, is the purest form of Indian music because, he argues, in such music there is no limitation of the geographical barrier of pronunciation or accent on the words, no injunction (so-called) of poetry. The musical notes here can freely swim across the ocean of music in their purity and sanctity. Perhaps in view of the predominant aspect of abstraction governing the entire domain of Indian music at different levels, Rabindranath is inspired by the height of abstraction which instrumental music alone can achieve. It is true not only in respect of Indian music but of music in general which is in quest of the highest abstraction in every possible way.

Regarding his songs it can be said that he has introduced a new type of *Deśi Sangeet* as different from what has been visualized by *Matanga*. The songs of Rabindranath can be classified under *Deśi Sangeet*, but with a difference. Rabindranath has given proper emphasis on the *rāgas* which normally constitute *Mārga Sangeet* as visualised by *Matanga*. So the songs of Rabindranath are *Deśi Sangeet* under the influence of *Mārga Sangeet*. These are much more sophisticated type than those which *Matanga* had in view. To understand this point let us refer to the observations of *Matanga*. As the first characterization of *Deśi Sangeet* we may refer to the following verse from *Bṛhaddesi*.

Abalābālagopālai kshitipālairnijechhayā
Geeyate Sānurāgena Svadeśe Deśiruchyate.

It reads: Those songs are called *Deśi* songs which are sung by women, boys, cowboys and kings according to their own loving affection and tender emotion in their respective countries (or places of residence).

As regards the second characteristic the following verse may be helpful:

Alāpādinibadhha ya sa ca Mārga Prakeertita
Alāpādibiheenastu sa ca Deśi Prakeertita.

It reads: *Mārga* songs are those which are bound by *ālāpa* and its cognates; *Deśi* songs are those which are free from *āḷāpa* and its cognates.

From these two characteristics it follows that *Deśi* songs are those which are free from any elaboration of notes with the help of *ālāpa* (a technical term in Indian musicology where a *rāga* is made elaborate by free interplay of the notes, free in the sense that it is not set to any definite rhythmic pattern normally rendered by percussion instruments; still it is said to have a dormant, natural rhythm of its own), and sung freely according to one's emotion and not according to the rules or conventions prescribed for any definite melody-pattern. Such *deśi* songs are said to constitute the vast domain known as folk-music.

The chief merit of the musical creativity of Rabindranath is that he composes the melody of his lyrics in accordance with the general spirit of some definite traditional melody-patterns faithfully (in most of the cases) following the prescribed sequence of the notes. He is, however, careful enough not to introduce any *ālāpa* elaboration of his songs. The former, namely, the use of specific note-sequence of a *rāga* was totally absent in the *Deśi* songs as referred to by *Matanga*. It will be seen that most of the *rāgas* invented by the ancient musicologists could be traced to the melody of the *Deśi* songs. Talented and gifted musicians or musicologists, whenever came across any *deśi* song, immediately converted it into a richer melody and infused in it a system of note-sequence which subsequently took the form of a *rāga* or a definite melody-pattern. Most of the *rāgas* are said to be constituted in this way. Rabindranath, a versatile genius in all domains of art, takes the other course. He was fully acquainted with the *rāga* system of Indian music and with his literary gift composed the lyric and set it to the tune of one or other of the standard melodies according to the specific sentiment revealed by his poems. It is in this sense that he is said to have composed a new variety of *deśi* songs with much more sophistication and aesthetic refinement than can be found in ancient *deśi* songs. He has also clearly shown the four *tuks* in dividing his songs into *Sthāyi, Antarā, Sancāri* and *Ābhog*. Most of the ancient *deśi* songs could not be said to reflect the spirit of the standard melodies. Those were the pure innocent, spontaneous expression of the inner rhythm of the soul verbally illustrated with the help of a tune indigenous to the soil.

Melodies are constructed on the basis of such indigenous songs which, as if, showed the path of systematic construction of melody-pattern for those who knew the secrets of the specific art. Rabindranath, at a much later period, applied the standard melodies back to their original home and created his own songs as free from all technical elaborations or super-imposed improvisations. His melodies seem to have a universal appeal even to those who are not acquainted with musicological details. The appeal is due to the unique combination of lyric and melody, both flowing from the same aesthetic appeal. The selection of the suitable melody patterns makes his songs a glorious and crowning success in the history of Indian music where one readily sees how the standard of Indian melodies in the hands of a master musician can be put to use where not the technicality but the inner spirit reigns supreme. The lyric and the melody in Rabindranath complete each other.

Ālāpa in Indian music is by definition content-free. The treatment of a *rāga* with the help of *ālāpa* is perhaps an unparallel asset of Indian music, and here also it reaches the highest level of abstraction because it goes beyond any verbal articulation of feelings and sentiments. Rabindranath being committed to his poems has to abandon the aspect of *ālāpa* in his songs and this is all for the better. He wanted to create a new horizon of *deśi* songs which could be able to touch the heart and soul of mankind free from any training or lessons in musical technicalities or theories.

The aspect of improvisation which is another unparallel asset of Indian music is meant chiefly for aesthetic ornamentation or for constructing a vast aesthetic super-structure by permutation and combination of serveral notes in a disciplined and proportionate way. Supreme aesthetic embellishment is achieved no doubt; but the main objective of Rabindranath happens to be to reveal the subtle and delicate sentiments as recorded in his poems with the help of music and to create aesthetic super-structures which are lyric-bound. He believes that music is more eloquent than verse, and so he chooses to create the melodies through which his poems could expectedly reveal better their own feelings which in turn are intrinsically the feelings of the poet himself. He is the sole arbiter as regards the medium of expression of his spiritual vision. So he chooses to combine both and this opens the new horizon and establishes the point beyond dispute that Indian music is ever progressive, ever creative. There is no end to it, a path of eternal quest.

Initially trained under the leading exponents of *Visnupur gharānā*, the versatile genius could not be made confined to the conventional features and styles of the *gharānā*. In course of time, the spiritual vision with which he was gifted right from his birth, his intrinsic treasure took him to the new and untrodden path of creating music in a style exclusively his own. Apart from the standard melodies of ancient and traditional Indian music, from which he has derived his whole inspiration of music, he has made full use of the immense depth of the indigenous melodies like *Bāul, Keertan, Bhātiyāli, Tappā, Rāmprasādi* and what not. In his treatment of traditional melodies one can find frequent but very appropriate use of two *rishavas*, two *dhaivatas* and other deviations not recommended by the orthodox musicological system. This has not destroyed the aesthetic appeal of his lyrics, nor the appeal of his melody, nor even the appeal of the *rāgas* themselves of which he has taken only the suitable, appropriate shades, suitable for reflecting his own vision. Like a perfect master with a deep insight and mature imagination enriched with aesthetic vision he has created a melody which is a meeting-point of the current, modern and ancient ones in music in all directions.

It is in this sense that one would find a justification of his view that musicological injunctions should not always be rigidly followed. What, in its place, should be rigidly followed is the law of intrinsic necessity, the inner spiritual realization of man, the spontaneous aesthetic verdict, and then, and then alone music will have its course in all directions of newer and richer creativity. The traditional orthodox musicological rules and conventions must be given their due importance in view of the precious wealth of the universe of basic *rāgas* and their derivatives. This is, in other words, the source treasure of the music of India even in present days. In fact, the ancient orthodox musicians in their turn derived their inspiration from unsophisticated *Deśi* songs and through hard labour and deep concentration built the magnificent towering kingdom of Indian music. Had there been no strict rules and measures for preserving this treasure, we would have been deprived of the rare richness of Indian music. And Rabindranath has unhesitantly acknowledged this in many of his remarks and observations. If we deny the importance of the rigorous rules, we have no solid basis to stand. His point, however, is not to make Indian music stagnant and prosaic by emphasising the exhibitionism in music; he, on the other hand, has tried his best to make new innovations on the basis of ancient musicological system and has made the music freely creative in other directions keeping in view the purity of the foundational aesthetic appeal.

To turn back to the point of improvisation, again. Improvisation in the context of Indian music is normally understood to convey the sense of aesthetic freedom of the musician in creating melodic super-structures with the help of *ālāpa* and *tān*. It shows the immense potentiality of the musician in showing how many diverse ways there can be for arranging, rearranging, moulding, remoulding the initially working notes of a given melody-structure within the structure itself, either in simple or in complicated networks. Such networks are very delicate, subtle and refined. There are various technicalities to be followed in improvising any given melody-pattern. These all belong to the practical aspect of Indian music which is equally a vast domain. Each of all the Indian melodies may be rendered with equal success for three minutes or for three hours or even for three consecutive days. Such is its potential richness in the hands of master performer. At every stage, the performer goes on spontaneously composing the networks, unforeseen but somehow unconsciously visualized. Instrumental music, in case of solo performance and not in case of accompaniment to a solo, is chiefly based on such improvisation. It is all abstract. Similarly abstract is the improvisation in case of vocal solo music which is performed as *ālāpa* in *Dhrupad* and *vistāra* with the help of *tān* in *Kheyāl*, the two principal forms of vocal music. In case of *vistāra* and *tān*, the vocal music becomes content-free. The use of lyric or content is confined only to the unfolding of the basic melody-pattern of the *rāga*, normally called the *sthāyi*. In some cases, the use of lyric may be extended to *antarā* also. But in *sancāri* or *ābhog* it again becomes lyric-free and abstract and is mainly confined to improvisation. Indeed, the different so-called *gharānās* of Indian music come into being mainly as a result of the different interpretations of the aspect of improvisation, and partly as a result of the specific style or technique of presentation as suited to the specific interpretation of improvisation.

Rabindranath has particularly drawn our attention to a kind of improvisation in vocal music which is not content-free or lyric-free and which is not connected either with *Dhrupad* or with *Kheyāl*. It is to be found in the very popular so-called folk-song prevalent particularly in undivided Bengal which is customarily described as *Keertan*. Here the singers freely improvise both the lyric and the melody which is technically called *ākhara*. The musicians, mostly in group songs, always, as a rule, go on spontaneously improvising the lyric, as connected with the basic theme of the starting lyric composition as the pointer, and spontaneously set the improvised lyric in excellent improvised melodies. This is perhaps one unique feature of improvisation in vocal music which is content-dependent.

If the notion of improvisation is associated with the notion of the freedom of musicians, then how can Rabindranath be allegedly said to be in favour of the former and not in favour of the latter? It is customarily held by the critics of Rabindranath that so far as his own songs are concerned he is not inclined to allow any freedom to those who would like to render his songs. The main thrust in such a criticism is this: Rabindranath in upholding the cause of abstraction in aesthetic enjoyment and consequently of abstraction in improvisation in respect to the rendering of *mārga sangeet* is very much in favour of the freedom of the musicians: moreover, he himself has fully exercised his freedom in deviating from the standard musicological injunctions in creating his own melodies. If such be the case, it is highly inconsistent that Rabindranath would prohibit any type of freedom in rendering his own songs.

There is indeed some weight in the above criticism. But the whole picture might be seen from a different angle. As regards music which is lyric-free or content-free there is no harm if the musician applies his own freedom resulting from his own realization. But when music is restricted to any lyric, it is expected that the melody should be strictly in accordance with the aesthetic appeal of the lyric. The conservative outlook of Rabindranath regarding his own songs may be defended by arguing that there is every possibility that the musician in applying his freedom might destroy the aesthetic appeal of his own lyrical composition. He has deviated from the ancient musicologists only in view of a richer creativity. If the musicians in rendering his songs can create something new and richer, then possibly he has nothing to oppose. But he is rather scared by the cases of under-trained musicians with a somewhat inferior sense of aesthetic values, and that is why he has become conservative as regards his own songs. But he is always in favour of new innovations only on condition that such innovations will open a new path for greater, richer and deeper aesthetic creativity. In short, freedom of the musicians is rather restrictive in cases of lyric-dependent music.

The musician who has got the proper key to unlock the doors of the innermost feelings of his soul can reach the secrets of his invaluable treasures. Here he will find the kingdom of pure joy and pure bliss. Rabindranath frankly confesses that *Tānsen* was successful in diving deep into this kingdom. Once this is attained, music flows spontaneously as being its own necessity. Then the musician does not have to follow any rule; on the contrary, rule follows his music.

The intrinsic vibration of the immense dynamism of music produces a radiance in our soul manifested in our emotive feelings which are never empirical. The intensity of vibration which is perpetually going on in cosmic creation has its counterpart within us in music. When we have an access to the intrinsic core of such radiant vibration within us, our music which is its spontaneous manifestation, takes us beyond the limitations of space and time, and invites the vast cosmic consciousness—the Infinity and the Eternity within our bosom and we get lost into it forgetting our own individuality. In this sense, it is said that Indian music with its spiritual foundation overflows national boundaries and ushers forth the eternal universal appeal.

Rabindranath firmly believes that the meaning of his songs is better understood through music than through the poems. In music it shines more brilliantly and perhaps more triumphantly. Master musicians, indeed, create new forms in music. Then come some musicians under whose misguided leadership it may be imprisoned in dark fetters. But again time comes when man breaks through the prison and goes ahead towards a glorious creation.

In Western music, the improvisation or variations are often previously prescribed by the composer himself. The performers only display with skill what has been prescribed. The outlook of Indian music is jüst the opposite. Nothing is prescribed; if anything is prescribed it is only some basic cryptic note-sequence and nothing else. Everything is the musician's own creation with a high standard of realization. According to Rabindranath, Western music has a comparative liberty about time (since it believes in free rhythm); but in Indian music there is freedom of melody with no freedom of time (since it believes in bound rhythm, bound by the *Sam*). The Indian musician with his creative outlook goes on interpreting by improvisation the general law of a given melody indefinitely but within the rhythm-bound circle. The measure of the musician's freedom is his own creative personality. Real music or classical music is not the interpretation of words; it is the interpretation of the melody. It is very subtle and intricate, and it creates a relatively complete world of melody by itself. Indian music is the finest example of individual taste conforming to the universal standard.

A similarity of approach between Rabindranath and Popper is also worth mentioning in this context. Popper, like Rabindranath, argues that established melodies give rise to innumerable richer melodic variations. A tradition of melodies opens to us a whole new ordered world, a new cosmos. It appears that Popper has in view the Indian music and its unfettered growth. Regarding Western music Popper[10] maintains:

> A dramatic oratorio such as Bach's *St. Mathew Passion* depicts strong emotions and thus, by sympathy, arouses strong emotions—stronger perhaps even than Beethoven's *Mass in D*. There is no reason to doubt that the composer felt these emotions too; but, I suggest, he felt them because the music which he invented must have made its impact on him (otherwise he would, no doubt, have scrapped the piece as unsuccessful), and not because he was first in an emotional mood which he then expressed in his music.

Popper in this connection refers to an inscription which runs as: "From the heart—may it again go to the heart." How beautifully and suggestively the spirit of Indian music has been portrayed by a Western philosopher in the context of Western music! As a matter of fact, one thing may be said that really good music whether of India or of Europe cannot be exhaustively analysed.

The musicological outlook of Rabindranath together with that of the ancient musicologists encourages us to compare the music of India to the swan, the only creature of the animal kingdom which can *walk, swim* and *fly*. It covers all the three hemispheres of this universe. It is in the potentiality of a swan that we find the meeting-point of the empirical and the transcendental, which is overall transcendentally inclined. It is in this transcendental direction and not in its empirical root that Indian music can be best and most adequately understood. Moreover, the whiteness of the swan speaks of purity and sanctity of all our values, which constitute their spiritual dimension.

Again, the analogy of swan is suggestive from another point of view. In Sanskrit, it is called *Haṃsa* and is understood to be the key-concept of the vital core of all human endeavours in spiritual pursuits. The analogy intended here is based on the natural instinct of a swan in its discriminatory partaking of the *essence* from among the accompanying accidental trivialities of any empirical situation. The essence helps the man to transcend the boundaries of the so-called empirical limitations and obstacles. This is possible not by any cognitive efforts, nor by any imaginative power alone, but by a dedication from within to the vital *impulse*, the irresistible, inexhaustible, intrinsic and ineffable upsurge characteristic of all human beings. It encircles the basic spiritual realization of man, his identity with the Supreme Great, the magnificent cosmic power in its perpetual creativity. *Swan* or *Hamsa* is the symbol of *Pranava*, the cosmic sound-potential as realized within one's vital core.

Music is the spiritual man's creativity. It is what keeps man free and perpetually creative. The essence is love and tranquillity of mind which enables man to always march forward in his musical creativity resting on the vibrating core of cosmic sound-potential and bursting forth in innumerable, ineffable creations of tone and melody.

In the language of Popper:[11]

> Thus musical and scientific creations seem to have this much in common: the use of dogma, or myth, as a man-made path along which we move into the unknown, exploring the world, both creating regularities or rules and probing for existing regularities. And once we have found, or erected, some landmarks, we proceed by trying new ways of ordering the world, new coordinates, new modes of exploration and creation, new ways of building a new world, undreamt of in antiquity unless in the myth of the music of the spheres.

This is indeed true of music as a whole, whether Indian or European.

Musical theories are thus man-made; but the musicians always want to impose them upon the world not as a means of their verification, but as means of changing the existing world, in their ceaseless attempt to create a new world with new rules governing it which are always open to new refinements by fresh experiments according to the law of man's intrinsic necessity, man's own spiritual realization. But Western music, in order to proceed in this line of visualization, has to come out of its prescriptive character of musical themes in fixed notational details of harmony.

To turn back once more to the musical vision of Rabindranath himself. The poet argues that something more is there in the sky of the dawn and its breeze which cannot be taken to be a *fact* or even to be a *matter of fact*. This something more, unanalysable and indescribable, is the *rasa* which can only be *felt*, the *felt whole in its immediacy*. It is through this world of *rasa* that there is the aesthetic union between ourselves and Nature; none of this duality can be understood in isolation from the other; in fact, one completes the other.

Bhairavi, according to Rabindranath, is, as it were, the eternal pining away of the Infinite in the pang of separation, embedded in the very heart of cosmic creation; *Bhairav* is, as it were, the very first awakening of the sky of dawn; *Paraj*, the sleepy languor of late night; *Kānāda* is, as it were, the trysty midnight missing her route in deep darkness; *Multān* is the weary breathing of the sun-blaze residuum of the afternoon; *Puravi* is the widowed evening, shedding tears while wandering alone in the void; *Deshmalhār* is, as it were, the gay murmur of the primordial spring spontaneously emanating from the fountainhead of tears.

These are some of the indications as to how the poet has visualized the ethos behind the *rāgas*. He firmly holds that all this makes our waking consciousness transcend the limits of our space and time and realize the ever-dynamic eternal flow of life against the perspective of the stupendous, the Great beyond us. When the *rāgas* in the hands of master-musicians come to a close for the time-being, they leave behind no trace of mathematical calculations in our pages of theory. There is no retreat from Indian music; it is always a progress ahead.

In conclusion it can be said that if the sounds of *SRGM* and those of the percussion instruments without any balance or proportion fall into our ears, we feel extremely fatigued and try our best to get rid of such a situation. But again within these sounds we can discover the shining music when they are proportionate and balanced. Then with such disciplined sound of notes we discover *within measure what is beyond measure*; *within the finite what is beyond finite*; *within the available what is beyond our reach*. Music is something which is beyond the exhibitionism of *SRGM* or the complicated *tāns* or the complicated *layas*; it is something ineffable, something which is somewhere hidden between the owned and the non-owned, which is not simply the tune, nor simply the rhythm or the note-sequence, but all blended into one, encompassing but at the same time transcending all these in their separateness. This is the music of India. And Indian musicology may be said to be rooted in the religion of man's spirituality, his vision in the transcendental direction of the basic realization of the aesthetic enjoyment as reflected in the melodic units along with the unending, ever-radiant improvised super-structure which is the intrinsic quest of man in his search for the Infinite.

NOTES AND REFERENCES

1. For a detailed treatment of the historical evaluation of the classification of *Rāgas* see O.C. Gangoly—*Rāgas & Rāginis*.
2. *Abhinava-rāga-manjari*: Poona, 1921 (as incorporated by O.C. Gangoly in his *Rāgas & Rāginis*: Appendix 36).
3. Pandit Bhātkhande is also no exception to this. There is no definite principle of classification on the basis of which one can justify his approach. He himself appears not to have given any.
4. The term 'blue-print' is taken here to convey the sense of 'finality' and exactness in full details.
5. The idea is borrowed from *Creative Unity*, p. 78.
6. *The World as Will and Idea*, pp. 336-337.
   References to E. Hanslick or to S. Langer have been avoided here because too much discussion has already been done by many scholars in this field.
7. The list of songs as the embodiment of specific *rasas* is borrowed from Prafulla Kumar Das—*Rabindra Sangeet Prasanga*, Vol. II.
8. *Ibid.*, p. 338.
9. For a detailed study of the cases of deviation from the standard interpretation of *Rāgas* see Santidev Ghosh—*Rabindra Sangeet*, p. 58. Dhurjati Prasad Mukherjee in his paper on 'Tagore's Music' as incorporated in the *Centenary Volume* of Rabindranath, 1861-1961 has suggested new names of such *rāgas* created by Rabindranath as *Rabindra Bhairavi*, *Rabindra Puravi*, *Rabindra Sarang* and so on; and he is quite optimistic that in course of time such names will be accepted by history because of the immense richness of the melodies which bear the marks of unique realization of Rabindranath himself.
10. K. Popper—*The Philosophy of K. Popper*, Autobiography, p. 49.
11. *Ibid.*, p. 45.

APPENDIX

A list of some important works on Musicology*

1. *Dattilam* by *Dattila*
2. *Nātyaśāstra* by *Bharata*
3. *Bṛhaddesi* by *Matanga*
4. *Sangeet Makaranda* by *Nārada*
5. *Sangeet Ratnamālā* by *Mammata*
6. *Nātya Locana* by *Nānyadeva*
7. *Hṛdayalaṅkāra* by *Nānyadeva Sarasvati*
8. *Mānosollāsa* by *Somesvara Deva*
9. *Sangeet Ratnākara* by *Sārangadeva*
10. *Sangeet-Samaya-Sāra* by *Pārsadeva*
11. *Rāgārnava* in *Sārangadhara Paddhati*
12. *Rāga Tarangini* by *Locana Kavi*
13. *Pancama Samhitā* by *Nārada*
14. *Ratnākara Teekā* by *Kallinātha*
15. *Sangeet Sāra* by *Harināyaka*
16. *Rāgamālā* by *Mesakarna*
17. *Māna-Kuthuhala* by *Rājā Mānsingh Tomār*
18. *Rāgamālā* by *Rājā Mānsingh Tomār*
19. *Rāgamanjari* by *Viththala*
20. *Svara-mela Kalānidhi* by *Rāmāmātya*
21. *Rāga-Vivedha* by *Somanāth*
22. *Sangeet Darpana* by *Hariballabha*
23. *Catur-Dandi-Prakāsika* by *Venkatamākhi*
24. *Sangeet Pārijāta by Ahovala*
25. *Anupa-Sangeet-Ratnākara* by *Bhava Bhātta*
26. *Sangeet Dāmodara* by *Subhankara*
27. *Sangeet Nārāyaṇa* by *Purusottama Misra*
28. *Abhinava Bhārati* by *Abhinava Gupta*
29. *Sangeeta Taranga* by *Rādhāmohon Sen*

*No claim is intended as regards the list either about its historical order or about its authenticity. It is customarily accepted to be a list of major original works on Indian musicology.

30. *Abhinava Rāg-manjari* by *Pandit V.N. Bhātkhande*
31. *Sangeet Kalānidhi* by *Siṃhabhupāla*
32. *Sangeet Raja* by *Mahārāṇā Kumbha*

[Hanumāna or Hanumat, described as Ãnjaneya, is considered to be a musical authority by Abhinava Gupta. The classification made by Hanumāna is said to be followed by Dāmodar Miśra, Hariballabha and many others. The school of Hanumāna is mentioned in *Tuphet-'ul-Hind* by Mahommed Rezzā Khān (1813).]

BIBLIOGRAPHY

Ānanda Bardhan & Abhinava Gupta—*Dvanyāloka-O-Locana*: tr. by Subodh Chandra Sengupta & Kalipada Bhattacharya (A. Mukherjee & Co., Calcutta, 1986)

Aurobindo, Sri—*The Foundations of Indian Culture* (Sri Aurobindo Library, New York City, U.S.A. 1972)

Barrett, D. and Gray, B.—*Treasures of Asia—Indian Painting* (Rizzoli International Publications, INC, N.Y. 1978)

Basu, Jogiraj—*India of the Age of Brahmanas* (Sanskrit Pustak Bhandar, Calcutta, 1969)

Basu, Manoranjan—*Tantras: A general study* (Sm. Mira Basu, Calcutta, 1976)

_______________ Fundamentals of the Philosophy of Tantras (Mira Basu Publishers, Calcutta, 1986)

Bandyopadhyaya, B.—*Rabindra Sangit: The Songs of Tagore* (Granthalaya Private Limited, Calcutta, 1981)

Bhattacharya, Arun—*A Treatise on Ancient Hindu Music* (K.P. Bagchi & Co., Calcutta, 1978)

Bhattacharya, K.C.— *Studies in Philosophy, Vols. I & II* (Edited by Gopinath Bhattacharya: Motilal Banarasidass, Delhi, 1983)

Bharat Muni—*Nāṭyasāstra* (edited by Suresh Chandra Bandyopadhyaya: Bengali translation assisted by Dr. Chhanda Chakravarty, Navapatra Prakashan, Calcutta, Vols. I, II, III, 1980, 1982, 1982)

Bhātkhande, V.N.—*A Comparative Study of Some of the Leading Music Systems*: English tr. (The Adyar Library: Madras, 1945)

Broadhouse, J.—*Musical Acoustics* (William Reeves, London, 5th impression)

Browning, R.—*A Selection of Poems: 1835-1864* (edited by W.T. Young, Cambridge University Press, 1929)

Buber, Martin—*The Philosophy of M. Buber*: ed. by P.A. Schilpp (Open Court, Illinois, 1967)

Chattopadhyaya, Sudhākar—*Reflections on the Tantras* (Motilal Banarasidass, Delhi, 1978)

Chowdhury, P.J.—*The Aesthetic Attitude in Indian Aesthetics* (The Journal of Aesthetics and Art Criticism. Fall 1965, Supplement to the Oriental Issue)

Cultural Heritage of India—The Ramakrishna Mission Institute of Culture, Golpark, Calcutta.
Vol. I—1937 (ed. by Suniti K. Chatterjee & others)
Vol. II —1937 (ed. by S.K. De & others)
Vol. III—1937 (ed. by Haridas Bhattacharya)
Vol. IV—1956 (")
Vol. V—1978 (ed. by Suniti Kumar Chatterjee)
Vol. VI—1986 (ed. by Priyada Ranjan Roy)

Coomaraswamy, A.K.—*The Dance of Shiva* (Sagar Publications, New Delhi, 1968)

________ *Time and Eternity* (Artibus Asiae Publishers, Ascona, Switzerland, 1947)

________ *Christian and Oriental Philosophy of Art:* Why exhibit works of Art (Dover Publications, U.S.A., 1956)

________ *History of Indian and Indonesian Art* (Dover Publications, U.S.A., 1965)

________ *Traditional Art and Symbolism* (edited by R. Lipsey, Princeton University Press, U.S.A., 1977)

Das, Prafulla Kumar—*Rabindra Sangeet Prasanga*, Vols. I & II (Jijnasa Publications, Calcutta, 1974)

Day, C.R.—*The Music and Musical Instruments of Southern India and the Deccan* (B.R. Publishing Corporation, Delhi, 1977)

Dudley, L. & Faricy, A.—*The Humanities* (McGraw Hill Book Co., U.S.A., 1960)

Durkheim, E.—*The Elementary Forms of Religious Life*: tr. by J.W. Swain (George Allen & Unwin, London, 1976)

Eliot, T.S.—*Notes Towards the Definition of Culture* (Faber & Faber, London, 1965)

Gamow, G. & Cleveland, J.M.—*Physics: Foundations and Frontiers* (Prentice Hall of India Ltd., New Delhi, Third edition, 1978)

Gangoly, O.C.—*Rāgas & Rāginis, Vol. I* (Munshi Ram Manohar Lal, New Delhi, 1948)

Golden Treasury—Selected and arranged by F.T. Palgrave (Oxford University Press, London, 1964)

Gautam, M.R.—*The Musical Heritage of India* (Abhinav Publications, New Delhi, 1980)

Ghosh, Nikhil—*Fundamentals of Rāga and Tāla* (Arun Sangeetalaya, Bombay, 1968)

Ghosh, Santidev—*Rabindra Sangeet* (Visva-Bharati, Calcutta, 1980)

Gupta, Monoranjan—*Rabindra Chitrakala* (Saraswati Library, Calcutta, 1949)

Huxley, J.—*Religion without Revelation* (Harper and Row, U.S.A., 1957)

Hospers, J. (ed.)—*Introductory Readings in Aesthetics* (The Free Press, N.Y., 1969)

Ibrahim Adilshah II—*Kitab-I-Nauras*: ed. Nazir Ahmad, Lucknow University, General Editor, Nirmala Joshi, Secretary, Sangeet Natak Akademi, Delhi (Bharatiya Kala Kendra, Delhi, 1956)

Joshi, B.—*Understanding Indian Music* (Asia Publishing House, Calcutta, 1963)

Kaufmann, W.—*The Rāgas of South India* (Oxford & IBH Publishing Co., Calcutta, 1976)

Kaviraj, Gopinath—*Sādhu Darsan-O-Satprasanga*—5 Vols. (Prachi Publications, Calcutta, 1983)

Kramrisch, S.—*Indian Sculpture* (Motilal Banarasidass, New Delhi, 1981)

Kunhan Raja, C.—*Sangeet Ratnākara of Sārangadeva*, English tr. (The Adyar Library, Madras, 1945)

Matanga Muni—*Bṛhaddeśi*: ed. Mangal Ramakrishna Telang (Trivandrum Edition, 1928)

Mitra, Rajyeswar—*Vaidik Aitihye Sāmgān* (Jijnasa, Calcutta, 1978)

____________ *Vedagāner Ritiprakriti* (Uttarsuri Prakashan, Calcutta, 1983)

____________ *Vedagāner Prakrita Rupa* (Maneesha, Calcutta, 1984)

Mode, Heinz—*Indian Folk Art* (Alpine Fine Arts Collection, N.Y. tr. by Peter & Ross, 1985)

Mukhopadhyaya, Dilip K.—*Bhāratiya Sangeete Gharānār Itihās* (A. Mukherjee & Co. Calcutta, 1978)

Mukhopadhyaya, M. (Ed.)—*Kavi Jayadeva-O-Sri Geeta Govinda* (Dey's Publishing, Calcutta, 1978)

Pandey, K.C.—*Comparative Aesthetics, Vol. I* (Chowkhamba Sanskrit Series, Varanasi, 1959)

Popper, K.—*The Philosophy of K. Popper*, Vols. I & II (ed. by P.A. Schilpp, The Open Court, Illinois, 1974)

Prajnanananda, Swami—*A History of Indian Music, Vol. I* (Ramakrishna Vedanta Math, Calcutta, 1963)

_____________ *Rāga-O-Rupa, 2 Vols.* (Ramakrishna Vedanta Math, Calcutta, 1961)

Robertson, R.—*The Sociology of Religion* (Penguin Education, 1972)

Roy Chowdhury, Birendra K.—*Hindusthāni Sangeete Tānsener Sthān* (Jijnasa Publications, Calcutta, 1981)

Russell, B.—*Why I am not a Christian* (Unwin Paperback, London, 1973)

Santayana, G.—*The Sense of Beauty* (Dover Publications, N.Y., 1955)

Sanyal, A.—*Vaidik Svara Rahasya* (Burdwan University, Burdwan, 1969)

Sārangadeva—*Sangeet Ratnākara*: ed. Suresh Chandra Bandyopadhyaya (Rabindra Bharati University, Calcutta, 1982)
English edition—Pandit S. Subrahmanya Sastri, The Adyar Library, Madras, Vol. I—1943, Vol. II—1959, Vol. III—1951, Vol. IV—53

Sartre, J.P.—*Existentialism and Humanism*: Tr. by P. Mairet (Methuen & Co., London, 1955)

___________ *Being and Nothingness* (Methuen & Co., 1976)

___________ *The Psychology of Imagination* (Methuen & Co., 1976)

Schopenhauer, A.—*The World as Will and Idea, Vol. I*, tr. Haldane and Kemp (Kegan Paul, London, 1844, Seventh edition)

Seal, B.N.—*The Positive Sciences of the Ancient Hindus* (Motilal Banarasidass, Delhi, 1958)

Sharpe, E.J.—*Comparative Religion: A History* (Gerald, Duckworth & Co., London, 1975)

Sullivan J.W.N.—*Beethoven* (Pelican Books. New York, 1960)

Swami Gambhirananda (ed.)—*Upanisad Granthabali,* 3 Vols. (Udbodhan Karyalaya, Calcutta, 1977)

Titchner, E.B.—*A Primer of Psychology* (Macmillan Co., London, 1940)

Tagore, Rabindranath —*The Religion of Man* (Unwin Books, London, 1975)

____________ *Gitanjali* (English translation with introduction by W.B. Yeats) (Macmillan, London, 1942)

____________ *Personality* (Macmillan, London, 1985)

____________ *Creative Unity* (Macmillan, London, 1980)

____________ *Sadhana* (Macmillan, London, 1979)

____________ *Chitralipi* (Visva-Bharati, Calcutta, 1940)

____________ *Rabindranath Tagore on Art and Aesthetics*: ed. Prithwish Neogy (International Cultural Centre, New Delhi, 1961)

____________ *Rabindranath Tagore—A Centenary Volume: 1861-1961*

(Sahitya Akademi, New Delhi, 1986)
____________ *Sangeet Chinta* (Visva-Bharati, Calcutta, 1966)
____________ *Sahitya* (Visva-Bharati, Calcutta, 1974)
Thalheimer, R.—*Reflections* (Philosophical Library, N.Y., 1972)
Tomas, V. (ed.)—*Creativity in the Arts* (Prentice Hall, N.J., 1964)
Vequaud, Y.—*The Art of Mithila* (Thames & Hudson, London, 1977)
Vivas, E. & Kriegar, M. (ed.)—*The Problems of Aesthetics* (Holt, Rinehart and Winston, U.S.A., 1963)
Whitehead, A.N.—*Religion in the Making* (University Press, Cambridge, 1927)
Wittgenstein, L.—*Note Books*: 1914-1916: tr. G.E.M. Anscombe, ed. Von Wright & Anscombe (Basil Blackwell, Oxford, 1961)

of man in music is the beginning which melts away in his revelation where the musician gets merged in his own music and the distinction between the musician and his music is forever lost in a higher union, the underlying principle of unity being the cosmic phenomenon of sound in its refinement and purification created by the musician himself through his self-realization.

NOTES AND REFERENCES

1. Santayana, G.—*The Senses of Beauty*, p. 33.
2. Coomaraswamy has raised a very pertinent question. Why exhibit works of Art?
3. Sartre, J.P.— *Existentialism and Humanism*, p. 35.
4. It will be argued later on that for perfect and pure music the issue of the listener is a non-issue and the role of listener is absolutely superfluous in the context of pure musical creativity.
5. Sartre, J.P.—*Existentialism and Humanism*, p. 56.
6. The terms are borrowed from K.C. Bhattacharya—*Studies in Philosophy*. This issue will be taken up in connection with his analysis of *Rasa*.
7. *Studies in Philosophy*, Vol. I, pp. 355-356.
8. *The Religion of Man*, p. 80.

INDEX